the Cape Cod Table

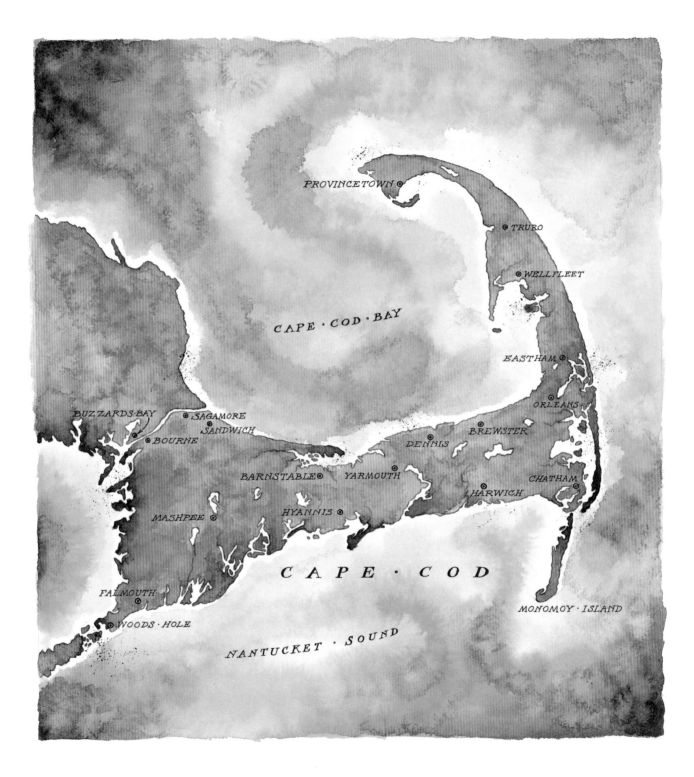

the Cape Cod Table

by **Lora Brody**

photographs by
Susie Cushner

The **Harvard Common Press**

Boston, Massachusetts

The Harvard Common Press
535 Albany Street
Boston, Massachusetts 02118
www.harvardcommonpress.com

Printed in China
Printed on acid-free paper

Special bulk-order discounts are available on
this and other Harvard Common Press books.
Companies and organizations may purchase
books for premiums or resale, or may arrange
a custom edition, by contacting the Marketing
Director at the address above.

Library of Congress Cataloging-in-Publication Data
Brody, Lora.
  The Cape Cod table / by Lora Brody ; photo-
graphs by Susie Cushner.
       p. cm.
  Originally pub.: San Francisco : Chronicle
Books, 2003.
  Includes index.
  ISBN 978-1-55832-366-7 (pbk. : alk. paper)
  1. Cookery, American--New England style. 2.
Cookery--Massachusetts--Cape Cod. I. Title.
TX715.2.N48B76 2007
641.5974--dc22

                              2007006499

Book design by Jana Anderson, studio A,
  San Francisco
Typesetting by Jana Anderson & Janis Reed
Prop styling by Helen Crowther
Food styling by Jee Levin

10 9 8 7 6 5 4 3 2 1

Photographer's Acknowledgment:
The magic of Cape Cod was experienced
in this project through the location, the
generosity of many Cape Cod "locals," and the
author, Lora Brody. As a native New Englander,
it was a pleasure to create the visual point of
view with perfect collaboration of my dear and
talented friend, Helen Crowther, who tirelessly
contributed her style, props, inspired eye, and
attitude; along with the natural and beautiful
food styling and expertise of Jee Levin. My assis-
tant, and friend, Meg Matyia, and to my sweet
Anna Wallack for keeping all the loose ends tied
up. I would also like to extend sincere gratitude
to all those amazingly generous people, who
extended assistance, locations, props, and even a
tripod, when needed: Jack Croucher, Bob
McCanant, Greg Saint Jean of Captain Jacks
Wharf, Caleb + Jason Almany, Richard Casey,
Brad Fowler, John Dowd, Sals's Place, and Paul
Endich. As always, these projects would not flow
so effortlessly without the consistant love and
loyalty from Judy, Teri, Jenna, and Kayla. Many
thanks to you all!

For David,

who continues to show me the way

& for Joanna and Max,

who are just starting out

acknowledgments

Grateful thanks to all my Cape Cod friends who have nurtured me and always made sure there was a place for me at the table: Mary, Alan, and Joanna Frankel; Joseph Polombo; Terry Catalano; Jay Coburn and John Guerra. To Liz Lovati and Alan Cullinane, the Angels at Angel Foods who made sure I never ran out of ingredients. To the talented crew at Provincetown Design Group, and especially the boss herself, my treasured friend Donna Vaillancourt, who graciously let me use her great line on page 19. Hats off to Paul and Tamara Endich for spoiling us with fantastic fudge. Thank you to Bob Prescott, Director of the Massachusetts Audubon Society Wellfleet Bay Sanctuary for information about herring runs. Thank you to Max Brody and Emmy Clausing for their help in creating and testing some of these recipes. Thank you to Mary Manning for transcribing the manuscript in record time and in perfect shape. Thanks to my wonderful neighbors on Thistlemore Road who make this end of town the best place to be. And last, but most certainly not least, thank you to my teachers at the Fine Arts Work Center in Provincetown, who inspire me to be the best I can be.

Contents

18 introduction

1 breakfast
28 Cape Cod Scones
29 The Best Blueberry Muffins
30 Blueberry Pancakes
33 Souffléd Apple Pancake
35 Cottage Street Bakery Dirt Bombs
37 Scrambled Eggs with Lox, Onions, and Peppers
38 Portuguese Muffins
40 Oatmeal Brûlée
41 Slow Cooker Oatmeal
42 Strawberries and Cream French Toast

2 appetizers
48 Baked Stuffed Clams
49 Irma's Clam Fritters
50 Quick White Bean and Garlic Dip
51 Classic Deviled Eggs
52 Fried Clams
54 Raw Bar
57 Boiled Shrimp
58 Scallop Seviche
60 Smoked Mussels
62 Smoked Salmon Cheesecake

3 soups and chowders
68 Kale Soup
70 Ginger Pumpkin Bisque
73 P. J.'s Fish Chowder
75 Clam Chowder
77 Oyster Stew
78 Saffron-Scented Cod and Tomato Soup
81 Bread Bowl Salmon Chowder

4 vegetables and salads
87 Dried Cranberry, Walnut, and Blue Cheese Salad
88 Cape Cod Turnips
89 Cape Corn and Rice Salad
90 Cauliflower Flans
91 Caramelized Onion Mashed Potatoes
92 Mac's Calamari Salad
94 Roasted Potatoes
95 Roasted Asparagus
96 Sunset Slaw
98 Two Salmon and Potato Salad

5 main courses
104 Grilled Pork with Cran-Asian Sauce
105 Grilled Flank Steak
106 New England Boiled Dinner
107 Roasted Chicken with Oyster Cracker Stuffing
108 Chicken Pot Pie
110 Cranberry Orange Turkey Breast
112 Grilled Brined Duck Breasts with Blackened Onion Relish
114 Millie's Oven-Fried Chicken
115 Grilled Bluefish with Mustard and Lime
116 Bacalhau (Portuguese Salt Cod)
117 Bacalhau with Fried Eggs
119 Cod Baked with Oven-Roasted Tomatoes
120 Broiled Gravlax
124 Sea Bass Poached in Ginger Fish Broth with Cilantro Pesto
127 Slow-Cooked Striped Bass
128 Baked Stuffed Lobster
130 Boiled Lobster
132 Lobster Rolls
133 Beer-Fried Oysters
134 Clambakes
    Outdoor Clambake
    Lazy Man's Clambake
138 Grilled Sea Scallops (Scallop Kabobs)
139 Leslie Revsin's Sautéed Cod with Capers
140 Mussels Three Ways
    Mussels Steamed with Wine and Garlic
    Bonfire Mussels
    Grilled Mussels
143 Steamed Clams
144 Spaghetti Foriana Ciro and Sal's
146 Spaghetti with White Clam Sauce
148 White Clam Pizza

6 desserts
155 Fresh Raspberry Blueberry Tart with a Shortbread Crust
156 Sand Dollars
158 Chocolate-Covered Cape Cod Potato Chips
160 Chocolate Mint Brownies
161 Mint Chip Brownie Ice Cream Sundae
162 Dune Cookies
164 Fresh Peach Ice Cream
165 Plum Kuchen
166 Quick and Easy Rocky Road Fudge
169 Lavender Crème Brûlée, Chester Restaurant
171 Mixed Berry Shortcake
172 Pumpkin Cheesecake
174 Cranberry-Pear Linzertorte

7 drinks
180 A Medley of Libations
    Sea Breeze
    Red Snapper
    Red Tide
182 Mulled Cider
185 Candy Manor Hot Chocolate
186 Cranberry Martini
189 Sun Tea

8 condiments
194 Beach Plum Jam
196 Bread and Butter Pickles
197 Cocktail Sauce
197 Tartar Sauce
198 The Green Briar Jam Kitchen
    Strawberry Jam
    Spiced Pear Jam
200 Cranberry Salsa
201 Lobster Butter
203 Oven-Roasted Tomatoes
204 Oven-Roasted Tomato Catsup
205 Pumpkin Cranberry Chutney
206 Quick Fish Stock
207 Simple Cranberry Sauce
208 Fresh Cranberry Orange Relish

212 index

216 table of equivalents

Introduction

From Bourne and Falmouth sitting on its muscular shoulder, to Harwich and Chatham clinging to its knobby elbow, to the slender fingertip of Provincetown, Cape Cod juts due east into the Atlantic before flexing its arm and casually pointing back toward the canal, cradling the bay that separates it from the mainland and everyday life. It is, as my friend Donna says, "a paradise conveniently located between sea and sky."

Fifteen puzzle-piece towns and villages fit together to form this singular sixty-mile peninsula. Each has its own distinct personality and, as a result, offers a menu of recipes and ingredients unique to this enchanted spit of sand.

Cape Cod has both its public and private culinary faces. While visitors who have braved the stop-and-go traffic and hair-raising rotaries to make it across the canal to Barnstable might make a beeline to one of dozens of clam shacks or the Dairy Joy, native "down Capers" know which hole-in-the-wall bakeries have just-made muffins laden with locally grown cranberries, where to find old-fashioned codfish cakes, and the ice cream stand that offers home-churned ice cream studded with tiny native strawberries. In Sandwich, despite its name, old-timers will tell you to forget your request for a turkey club and instead to search out the narrow path lined with wild iris that ends at the Green Briar Jam Kitchen, where members of the Thornton W. Burgess Society patiently stir vodka into copper vats of sun-dried Cape Cod blueberries and then spoon the heady mixture into waiting glass jars destined to be opened in midwinter by folks looking for a taste of summertime.

From Barnstable, Route 6A winds north to bayside Dennis—a good place to eat fried clams with a side of French-fried onion rings, washed down with a Sam Adams on draft, before turning south to the classic New England seaside towns of Harwich and Chatham.

Corn chowder, clam fritters, baked stuffed lobster, and strawberry shortcake are on the menu at veranda-wrapped inns and classic Cape restaurants with their views of the Chatham Lighthouse. Here you can choose to have the catch of the day grilled, broiled, poached, sautéed, or fried. Bed-and-breakfasts covered with climbing roses compete to serve the visitor the most comprehensive first meal of the day, but be forewarned: It's smart to save room for a piece of penuche fudge from the Chatham Candy Manor.

Leaving Chatham, the highway narrows as it winds northward to Orleans, which fronts on both Cape Cod and Pleasant Bays, as well as the Atlantic ocean. In wintertime, ice boats race over black ice-topped kettle ponds, and devotees (and observers) throw chili-filled foil-wrapped potatoes into the fires they've lit to warm their hands. The same ponds in summer offer swimming in crystal waters and the opportunity to work up appetites that are satisfied with home-grilled locally caught striped bass.

While the Cape has a bounty of great restaurants, Brewster on the bay side offers several that are nationally acclaimed for their elegant settings and their chefs' talents for turning local ingredients into exquisite haute cuisine. On a homier

note, roadside produce stands offer Cape Cod turnips, organic tomatoes, and ears of Butter and Sugar corn, along with bouquets of basil, thyme, and rosemary.

Wellfleet is famous for its oysters, briny and sweet and as fresh as the morning sun on calm water. Natives love them raw with a simple squeeze of lemon, but there is a strong case to be argued for trying them simmered in a simple stew of milk, cream, butter, and broth or fried up and tucked into a soft Italian roll spread with homemade tartar sauce. Here Route 6A is lined with open-air eateries offering buckets of steamers, lobster-in-the-rough, and fried clams worth writing home about. Sandy-from-the-beach families, sun-burned surfers, and local fishermen line up for lobster rolls and bowls of steaming New England clam chowder.

Tiny Truro offers miles of bay-washed flats inviting long, lazy strolls and plenty of opportunity for finding treasures in tide pools, as well as magically lit scenes that can be viewed in many of Edward Hopper's famous paintings. On the ocean side, men and women in waist-high waders trudge over dunes to cast out into the rolling surf in hopes of haul-ing in feisty bluefish and giant striped bass that will (if luck kisses the rod) be dinner on the table that night. Bonfires twinkle up and down the mist-shrouded oceanside beaches and light up the summer evening sky as friends and families gather for clambakes featuring lobster, steamers, corn on the cob, and cold beer, with thick slices of juicy watermelon for dessert.

Route 6A ends at Provincetown, the Pilgrims' first landfall. Fabulous, funky Provincetown, where worlds and cultures collide to create a stew of unforgettable ingredients and flavors. From the Portuguese fishing families offering kale soup with spicy chorizo, Portuguese sweet bread, and bacalhau (salt cod), to an international community of artists, writers, and poets along with some truly traffic-stopping characters, to a slew of trendy restaurants, each contributes local color and a delicious palette of flavors that scent the air with the enticing aroma of something special to eat. Whether it's my neighbor Bob's mussels with white wine and garlic, Mojo's famous cheese melts, a Red Tide (Cape Cod's take on a Bloody Mary) and a plate of seaweed salad at Clem and Ursie's, braised duck at the Martin House, or Chester's lavender crème brûlée, eating is an activity that goes on all day long and into the night. Some folks drive from the canal to Commercial Street in one hour, but there are those of us who know that a long, slow journey on back roads will bring the opportunity to savor each and every tasty morsel the Cape has to offer.

My husband-to-be brought me to Cape Cod on our first date in 1963. He took me first to Eastham, where every year of his childhood his parents rented a rustic cottage that backed onto a vast marsh overlooking First Encounter Beach, the place where in November 1620 the newly arrived Pilgrims had their first face-to-face meeting with what were most likely members of the Nauset tribe. On that brilliant spring afternoon, where you could look across the vast flat bay and see Plymouth hovering above the horizon, buffeted by winds off the land, seagulls wheeling and screaming at the solitary interlopers, we walked the flats at low tide. He showed me how to look into a tide pool and see hermit crabs and starfish, the telltale tiny bubbles a submerged clam leaves on the surface of the mud, and how horseshoe crabs look like (and are) remnants of a prehistoric time. We hiked the dunes and trails of the National Seashore made up of almost 44,000 acres saved forever from development and open to the public by the foresight of John F. Kennedy, whose family compound can be glimpsed over a high wall in Hyannisport. And so I began to fall in love with both this man who had driven me several hundred miles to see if I shared his passion for the sea and this isolated place of water, sand, and wind.

Later that day he took me to Provincetown, where even in the off-season, all hell was breaking loose, and pointed out that the only brick house in town was owned by Norman Mailer and told me that the tall blond woman in the slinky red dress, fishnet stockings, and spike heels was really a guy. He took me to the Mayflower Café, its high windows steamed with the cozy warmth inside, and fed me kale soup, thick with tomatoes and black beans and spiked with the heat of Portuguese sausage, and I knew that I had found a place where I could be very, very happy. "What a deliciously crazy place," I told him. "I could definitely see myself living here." He smiled indulgently.

It was thirty-six years before we bought our Provincetown dream house, which sits high on a wind-blown hill, and from which you can see the bay, the sweeping dunes, and the ocean, but every summer and many falls and winters before we bought the house we came to the Cape, sometimes just for an overnight, but more often for weeks at a time. When our children were small we rented bayside cottages in Eastham, Brewster, and Truro. When they became strong swimmers and learned to surf, we rented creaky, sand-filled shacks on the ocean.

Our Cape days are nourished by eccentrically wonderful neighbors, visits from friends, and simple meals made from the bounty of local ingredients. And not just the ingredients the whole world associates with Cape Cod: cranberries,

lobster, and cod, but spring herring that spawn in freshwater ponds and streams before making their way to the ocean, bluefish, striped bass, tuna, and flounder; cherrystone and steamer clams, quahogs, mussels, oysters, and periwinkles. We use native corn to make chowder and zucchini, tomatoes, pumpkins, and turnips for soups, stews, and salads. When the days shorten and summer nights turn cool, we make jam from native raspberries, blackberries, and blueberries and jelly from Concord grapes, wild beach plums, and lavender. We pick rose hips for tea and recklessly forage through poison ivy and thorny brambles to fight redwing blackbirds for the juiciest black raspberries that (if any are left in the pail after the picker has her fill) will go into pies, scones, and the world's most extravagant ice cream.

The recipes in this book reflect not only my dearly held associations and memories of seasons past, but also the mood that comes upon me as I drive over the bridge, anticipating precious time to walk the beaches, the woods, and the meadows of the Cape. Time to wade in the warm waters of the bay and to ride the crazy waves of the ocean. Time to be alone to create with both words and ingredients and, most important of all, time to share this place I love so well with friends and family. The breeze that carries the salt air and the scent of wild roses stokes pangs of hunger, and the bounty of the Cape is there to satisfy it.

1 breakfast

I love the way my family never has time for breakfast unless we're at the Cape. At home they rush out the door, mouthing empty promises to eat something when they get to work or school. When we're in Provincetown, however, they wander into the kitchen sometime before noon with hopeful looks on their faces, sniffing the air in expectation of something other than a bowl of cereal. Fortunately, the cook on duty (usually me) feels much the same way. The idea that there is actually time to sit down and have a real breakfast is one of the special things about being away from work and school and the pressures of everyday life.

Recipes that can fall (or be guided) into the category of breakfast are many. There are, of course, the classic, traditional foods such as eggs over easy, hot cereal, and pancakes with real maple syrup. And then there is a whole category of brunch dishes that promise to keep even the most famished eater sated until dinnertime. Whether you make Strawberries and Cream French Toast; Scrambled Eggs with Lox, Onions, and Peppers; or The Best Blueberry Muffins served hot from the oven, know that you will have an appreciative audience of devoted breakfast lovers just waiting to dig in and enjoy. By the way, we have a rule on the Cape—the cook never has to wash dishes.

Cape Cod Scones

Makes 12 scones

These can be made ahead, cooled completely, and then frozen for up to 2 months, wrapped individually in plastic wrap and then stored in a freezer-strength plastic bag. Pop them into a warm oven or toaster to heat when you are in the mood for something elegant to serve with afternoon tea.

If you have the urge, you can add some dried berries, but I know hard-liners in the United Kingdom—where scones originated—would disapprove. In our house we like them plain smeared with lots of butter and beach plum jam (page 194).

2	cups all-purpose flour, measured after sifting
1	tablespoon baking powder
³/₄	teaspoon salt
¹/₃	cup granulated sugar
¹/₂	cup dried berries of your choice, such as blueberries, cranberries, or strawberries (optional)
1¹/₄	cups heavy cream
3	tablespoons unsalted butter, melted
	Coarse sugar for sprinkling on tops

Preheat the oven to 425°F, with the rack in the center position. The scones will bake on an ungreased heavy-duty baking sheet. Into a medium-sized mixing bowl, sift the flour, baking powder, salt, and sugar. Use a table fork to mix well. If you are adding dried berries, stir them in at this point. Dribble the cream over the dry ingredients while mixing with the fork. Continue mixing gently just until the mixture forms a rough, sticky ball of dough.

Turn the dough out onto a lightly floured work surface, sprinkle lightly with flour, and knead 10 times by pushing the half closer to you down and away from you with the heel of your hand and folding it back over itself, giving it a quarter turn each time.

Pat the dough into a 9-inch disk. Brush the top with melted butter and sprinkle generously with coarse sugar. Use a long knife to cut the dough into 12 wedges and transfer each to the baking sheet, leaving about 1¹/₂ inches between them. Bake for 15 to 17 minutes, or until the tops are golden brown.

Serve warm or at room temperature.

The Best Blueberry Muffins

Makes 12 regular or 6 jumbo muffins

Midsummer at the Cape finds low-lying blueberry bushes almost sagging under the weight of ripe berries. Picking their own blueberries to make homemade blueberry muffins is something children love to do. This is a recipe that they can make with some supervision, especially around the oven. Making these by hand without the use of an electric mixer ensures that the finished muffins will be light and tender.

For the muffins

- 2 cups all-purpose flour
- 1 cup granulated sugar
- 2 teaspoons baking powder
- ½ teaspoon salt
- 2½ cups fresh blueberries, rinsed and shaken dry in a sieve, or 2½ cups slightly thawed frozen blueberries
- 2 extra-large eggs
- ½ cup milk
- ½ cup (1 stick) unsalted butter, melted and slightly cooled
- 2 teaspoons pure vanilla extract
  Finely grated zest of 1 medium orange

For the topping

- 3 tablespoons granulated sugar
- ½ teaspoon ground cinnamon
- ½ cup finely chopped walnuts

Preheat the oven to 400°F, with the rack in the center position. Line either a 12-cup muffin tin or a 6-cup jumbo muffin tin with fluted paper liners, or coat the cups and flat part of the tins generously with butter.

Sift the flour, sugar, baking powder, and salt into a medium-sized mixing bowl. Place 1 cup of the blueberries in another bowl and use a fork to mash them roughly.

Add the eggs to a larger mixing bowl and whisk to break them up. Whisk in the milk, melted butter, vanilla, and orange zest. Use a wooden spoon or rubber spatula to fold in the mashed berries. Fold the liquid mixture into the dry ingredients, mixing just to combine. There should be some dry lumps showing. Scrape the sides and bottom of the bowl to combine all the dry ingredients. Gently, fold in the whole blueberries.

Spoon and scrape the mixture into the prepared pans without smoothing the tops, filling them slightly more than halfway. Make the topping by mixing the sugar, cinnamon, and nuts together in a small bowl. Sprinkle generously over the batter. Bake the regular-sized muffins for 18 to 20 minutes and the jumbo muffins for 22 to 24 minutes, or until the tops are golden brown and a cake tester or toothpick inserted in the center comes out clean and dry. Let the muffins cool in the pan for 15 minutes before turning them out onto wire racks to cool completely.

Blueberry Pancakes

Makes about sixteen 6-inch pancakes or about sixty silver-dollar pancakes

The taste of hot blueberries exploding through tender, sweet pancakes is enough to make me wish for breakfast any time of day. The best test of a great breakfast joint is the quality of its blueberry pancakes—they have to be golden brown, light as a feather, full of the plumpest, juiciest, sweetest blueberries, and—this is almost the most important factor—fully cooked throughout. How often have you been served pancakes that are raw and wet in the middle? The trick to avoiding this is to make the batter with just enough liquid so that it spreads into a pancake that is thin enough to cook through. Feel free to adjust the batter by adding more milk so that it flows off the ladle like thick cream. The other trick is to make sure the pan is made of heavy-gauge metal that conducts heat well and evenly and that the pan is heated up completely before cooking.

This recipe can be cut in half, or you can mix up the dry ingredients and just use half, saving the rest (in a reclosable plastic bag in the freezer) for another time.

Here in New England we take our maple syrup very seriously. Yes, the price is (much) higher than imitation maple syrup, but the tastes aren't even in the same stratosphere. Please, please don't desecrate these wonderful pancakes by serving them with margarine and fake syrup.

3   cups all-purpose flour

1/3   cup granulated sugar

1/3   cup cornmeal

1   tablespoon baking powder

1   teaspoon salt

3   cups milk (or buttermilk for a slightly tangy, even more tender result), more if needed

6   tablespoons butter, melted and slightly cooled

3   extra-large eggs

1   tablespoon pure vanilla extract

2   cups fresh blueberries, rinsed only if necessary, shaken dry in a colander

     Butter for cooking the pancakes

     Butter and pure maple syrup for serving

continued on next page

In a pinch, commercial pancake and waffle mix works just fine—especially when you add enough blueberries.

Place the flour, sugar, cornmeal, baking powder, and salt in a mesh sieve set over a large mixing bowl. Shake the contents into the bowl. Place the milk, melted butter, eggs, and vanilla in a second bowl and whisk to combine. Pour the wet ingredients into the dry and gently stir until the mixture is smooth, taking care not to overmix, as this will make the pancakes tough. Add more milk, if necessary, to make a batter that is the consistency of thick heavy cream. Gently fold in the blueberries with a rubber spatula.

Melt a tablespoon of butter (or more if necessary) to cover the bottom of a large griddle or frying pan set over moderate-high heat. When the butter sizzles, ladle batter onto the griddle to form 6-inch pancakes, leaving enough room between them to let them spread without touching. Cook until bubbles form on the top of the pancake and the bottoms are golden brown. Use a wide metal spatula to flip them over, and cook on the other side until golden brown. Stick the point of a small, sharp knife into the center of one of the pancakes to make sure it has cooked all the way through. This will help you gauge the required cooking time. Repeat with the remaining batter.

You can keep the pancakes warm on a baking sheet, loosely covered with foil, in a 300°F oven.

Serve hot with lots of butter and real maple syrup.

Souffléd Apple Pancake

Serves 4

If you want to knock the socks off folks at the breakfast table, you've come to the right recipe. A sweet version of Yorkshire pudding, this oven-baked pancake puffs up and creates an envelope for tender slices of spiced apple. You can substitute fresh peach slices for the apples, if you wish.

Start with the batter and make the filling while the pancake bakes.

For the pancake

3	large eggs
¾	cup whole milk
¾	cup all-purpose flour
1	teaspoon salt
1½	tablespoons unsalted butter

For the filling

6	tablespoons unsalted butter
⅓	cup (packed) light brown sugar
	Juice and finely grated zest of 1 lemon
3	large, firm flavorful apples, such as Granny Smith or Gala, peeled, cut in half, cored, and sliced into ¼-inch wedges
½	teaspoon ground cinnamon
½	teaspoon ground ginger
	Confectioners' sugar for dusting

To make the pancake: Preheat the oven to 450°F, with the rack in the upper third of the oven, but not the highest position. In a medium-sized mixing bowl, stir or whisk together the eggs, milk, flour, and salt until smooth. Melt the butter in a large, ovenproof skillet set over high heat. When it sizzles, pour in the batter and immediately place the pan in the oven. Bake for 12 minutes, then reduce the oven temperature to 350°F and bake for another 10 minutes. The pancake will puff up dramatically. Pierce the bubbles with the tip of a sharp knife just to deflate it. The pancake should be light golden brown with crisp edges.

Make the filling while the pancake cooks, or make it ahead and hold it at room temperature for up to 8 hours in a covered container. Melt the butter in another large skillet set over high heat and add the sugar, lemon juice, and zest. Stir until the sugar melts, then add the apple slices and cook over moderate heat for 10 minutes. Sprinkle the cinnamon and ginger over the apples.

To serve the pancake: As soon as the pancake has finished cooking, slide it onto a heated oval platter. Spoon and scrape the apple filling over one half of the pancake, then use a wide metal spatula to fold the other half over the filling. Sift confectioners' sugar on top and serve immediately by cutting into wedges.

Cottage Street Bakery Dirt Bombs

Makes 12 "muffins"

One morning I wandered into the kitchen and found a white paper bag with the top scrunched closed sitting on the counter. I could tell it most likely had something good to eat inside from the butter stain on the outside—a dead giveaway. Inside there was half of what seemed to be a round ball that might have been second cousin to a doughnut. It sure smelled like a cinnamon-sugar doughnut to me. But it was substantially heavier than any doughnut I'd ever come across, more the heft of a muffin. Innocently I reached in, broke off a piece, and popped it into my mouth.

"Who is responsible for bringing this into my house!!???" I yelled, waking up my son and his girlfriend, who appeared in the kitchen faster than usual to find me holding the now empty bag, angrily wiping buttery crumbs from my mouth.

"Gee, we thought you'd like it," they chorused with concern.

"That's the problem. I do like it. I love it and now I'm hooked," I said. "I can't decide whether to yell at you for turning me on to these or to be mad that you only left me a half."

Welcome to the Cottage Street Bakery, where owner/baker Joanna Keeley works magic with butter, eggs, and flour and makes, among many other mouth-watering treats, the famous Dirt Bombs. If you are looking to lay off the sweet, rich stuff and have sworn off butter and sugar, then stop reading now. However, if you are in the mood for a quick trip to heaven, and you aren't close enough to drive to Orleans to the Cottage Street Bakery, don't wait another minute! Get out those muffin tins and crank up the oven—paradise awaits.

For the muffins

3	cups all-purpose flour
1	tablespoon baking powder
1/2	teaspoon salt
1/2	teaspoon ground nutmeg
1/4	teaspoon ground cardamom
3/4	cup (1 1/2 sticks) unsalted butter
1	cup granulated sugar
2	large eggs
1	cup whole milk

continued on next page

For the topping

¾ cup (1½ sticks) unsalted butter, melted

½ cup granulated sugar

1½ teaspoons ground cinnamon

Preheat the oven to 400°F, with the rack in the center position. Generously coat a 12-cup standard muffin tin with butter, greasing the flat part of the tin as well.

To make the muffins: Sift the flour, baking powder, salt, nutmeg, and cardamom into a mixing bowl. In a separate bowl, either by hand or using an electric mixer, cream the butter and sugar until light and fluffy. Mix in the eggs. Add the dry ingredients alternately with the milk in two additions, mixing gently by hand to incorporate all the ingredients. Scrape down the sides and bottom of the bowl to be sure to incorporate all the flour. The batter will be on the stiff side, but airy. Don't overmix or beat the batter, as this will make the muffins tough.

Scrape and spoon the batter into the prepared muffin tin without smoothing the tops. Bake for about 25 minutes, or until the tops are golden brown and a toothpick or cake tester inserted in the center comes out clean and dry. As soon as the muffins are cool enough to handle, turn them out onto a wire rack.

To coat the muffins with topping: Add the melted butter to a shallow bowl and mix the sugar and cinnamon together in a separate bowl. Dip the muffins (top, sides, and bottom) in the butter, using a pastry brush, if necessary, to cover areas not buttered by dipping. Immediately roll the muffins in the cinnamon-sugar mixture. Serve warm or at room temperature.

Scrambled Eggs with Lox, Onions, and Peppers

Serves 4

Some folks prefer their smoked salmon (lox, in our house) on a bagel with a schmear (a spread with cream cheese, for those of you who haven't lived in New York). I prefer mine scrambled up with some eggs, caramelized onions, and red and green bell peppers thrown in for color and texture. You can sauté the vegetables the night before and keep them at room temperature in a covered container; then this breakfast or brunch dish will take as long to make as it will for someone to set the table.

If you can find lox bits (scraps left over from hand-sliced smoked salmon), you can put the money you save toward your next Cape Cod vacation.

3   tablespoons unsalted butter

1   tablespoon vegetable oil

1   large Vidalia or other sweet onion, such as Maui, or Texas 10-15, peeled and cut into medium dice

1   small green bell pepper, cut in half, seeded, cored, and cut into ¼-inch dice

1   small red bell pepper, cut in half, seeded, cored, and cut into ¼-inch dice

10 large or extra-large eggs

¼   cup heavy cream, light cream, or whole milk

½   teaspoon freshly ground black pepper

½   teaspoon salt (omit if the salmon is very salty)

8   ounces smoked salmon, cut into ½-inch pieces

    Tabasco sauce

Heat the butter and oil in a large sauté pan set over moderate heat. Sauté the onion and both bell peppers, stirring occasionally, until the onion is light golden brown and the bell peppers are soft. Break the eggs into a mixing bowl and add the cream or milk and pepper; whisk to combine. Since the lox is salty, you may not need additional salt. Turn the heat up under the pan to high and when the butter sizzles, add the eggs and whisk to combine. Stir in the lox and pour the mixture into the hot pan. Stir gently with a heatproof plastic spatula or a wooden spatula, scraping the bottom and sides of the pan. The eggs should cook in a matter of minutes and should be quite soft. If cooked too long, they will get tough and watery. As soon as the eggs are set, divide them among 4 heated plates and serve immediately, passing the Tabasco sauce, accompanied by pumpernickel toast or toasted bagels.

Portuguese Muffins

Makes 10 large muffins

Portuguese muffins can best be described as English muffins made out of challah or a light brioche. While they are perfectly wonderful at breakfast when toasted and spread with a generous amount of jam, I love to use them to make both tuna salad and grilled cheese sandwiches.

This recipe is courtesy of King Arthur Flour test kitchen director Sue Gray, who spends a much-looked-forward-to week each summer in Wellfleet.

The potato and soy flour, though optional, contribute to the muffins' soft, tender texture. Both are usually available in the baking sections of supermarkets and health food stores, or you can order them from King Arthur by going to their Web site, www.kingarthurflour.com, or by calling 800-827-6836.

1	cup whole milk*
¼	cup (½ stick) unsalted butter, at room temperature
3½	cups unbleached all-purpose flour
¼	cup potato flour (optional)
¼	cup soy flour (optional)
¼	cup granulated sugar
2½	teaspoons active dry yeast
1½	teaspoons salt
2	extra-large eggs
2	teaspoons pure vanilla extract
⅛	teaspoon lemon oil, or 1 tablespoon finely grated lemon zest

*If you choose not to use the potato flour and/or soy flour, reduce the milk by 1 tablespoon.

To make the dough by hand: Scald the milk (heat it just until small bubbles form), then pour it over the butter in a small bowl. Set the mixture aside to cool to lukewarm.

In a large bowl, or in the bowl of an electric mixer, combine the flour(s), sugar, yeast, and salt, whisking thoroughly. (This prevents the potato flour from lumping.) Add the remaining ingredients, including the milk/butter mixture, mixing to form a workable dough. Knead the dough until it's smooth; this should be a soft (though not sticky) dough. Place the dough in a lightly greased bowl, cover the bowl with plastic wrap, and allow to rise for about 90 minutes; it'll become quite puffy.

To make the dough in a bread machine: Scald the milk (heat it just until small bubbles form), and then pour it over the butter in a small bowl. Set the mixture aside to cool to lukewarm.

Place all of the ingredients, including the milk/butter mixture, into the pan of your bread machine, program the machine for manual or dough, and press Start. About 10 minutes before the end of the final kneading cycle, examine the dough, and adjust its texture as necessary with additional flour or water. The dough should have formed a smooth, cohesive ball. Allow the machine to finish its cycle.

To shape and bake the muffins: Transfer the dough to a lightly oiled work surface, and divide it into 10 pieces, each about 3 ounces in weight. Form the dough into tight balls and let them rest, covered, for about 30 minutes. Flatten the balls into circles 4 to 5 inches in diameter and about $^1/_2$ inch thick.

Place the muffins on a lightly greased or parchment-lined baking sheet, leaving about $1^1/_2$ inches between them. Now, you're going to place a second baking sheet atop the muffins, in order to keep their texture fairly dense as they rise. Place a piece of parchment paper over the muffins, or lightly grease the bottom of the second baking sheet. Place the second sheet on top of the muffins, and let them rise for 45 minutes, or until they're about $^3/_4$ inch thick.

Preheat the oven to 400°F, with the rack in the center position. Bake the muffins for 18 to 22 minutes, leaving the second baking sheet in place; this will help keep the muffins flat. Remove the top baking sheet and test to make sure the muffins are done; they'll be golden brown on the top and bottom, with paler sides. Remove them from the oven, and cool on wire racks.

Oatmeal Brûlée

Serves 6

If you have overnight guests and wish to fix them a hearty breakfast without a whole lot of work, here's the perfect solution. You can make this with any sort of cooked oatmeal, instant, quick, or regular. My choice would be Irish oatmeal, which delivers a more interesting texture and wholesome taste. A recipe for making oatmeal overnight in the slow cooker follows.

1   cup (packed) dark brown sugar

¼   cup hot water

8   cups hot, cooked oatmeal, made according to package directions

4   large, firm bananas, peeled and sliced slightly on the diagonal in 1-inch ovals

      Milk (whole or low-fat) or light cream

Preheat the broiler with the rack in the upper third of the oven. Select 6 broilerproof bowls and place them on a heavy-duty rimmed baking sheet. In a small bowl, mix the brown sugar together with the water to make a thick paste. Divide the oatmeal among the bowls. Arrange the bananas in a fan shape on top of the oatmeal. Divide the brown sugar mixture among the bowls, and use the back of a spoon to spread it to cover the bananas. Place the baking sheet under the broiler and broil for 3 to 4 minutes, or until the brown sugar starts to bubble. Cook only until the entire surface is bubbling, but not so long that the sugar begins to burn. Remove from the broiler and serve hot, passing milk or cream on the side.

Slow Cooker Oatmeal

Makes about 8 cups

If you own a slow cooker and you would rather sleep late and find your hot cereal ready and waiting, this recipe is for you.

2½ cups regular oats (not quick cooking or instant)

8 cups water

2 teaspoons salt

2 tablespoons butter (optional)

1 cup golden or dark raisins (optional)

Place all the ingredients in a slow cooker (Crock-Pot) and stir to combine. Cook on High for at least 4 hours, or overnight on Low. It is not necessary to lift the lid to stir during the cooking time or to add water unless the oatmeal is very thick.

Leftover oatmeal is a great addition to bread dough (add 1 cup cooked oatmeal for every 4 cups of flour). You will have to adjust the amount of water in the bread to account for the water in the oatmeal. Cooked oatmeal also makes a great addition to poultry stuffing.

Strawberries and Cream French Toast

Serves 6

I often use Portuguese sweet bread in this recipe to make something a little novel to serve for brunch—especially if I want my family's and/or guests' hunger sated until dinner. Two slices of rich egg bread are dipped in egg batter and pan-toasted, then filled with sweetened cream cheese and finished in the oven. The strawberry topping is the icing on the cake. This dish can be made ahead up to the point where it goes in the oven.

For the French toast

 4   large or extra-large eggs

 ¾   cup whole milk

 1   tablespoon pure vanilla extract

 12 slices challah, Portuguese sweet bread, or other rich egg bread, cut into 1-inch slices

 ¼   cup (½ stick) unsalted butter, more if needed

For the filling

 6   ounces regular cream cheese (not whipped, low-fat, or nonfat), at room temperature

 ⅓   cup granulated sugar

     Finely grated zest of 1 large orange

 2   tablespoons Grand Marnier or other orange liqueur or brandy, or 3 tablespoons orange juice

For the strawberry sauce

 10 ounces frozen strawberries in syrup, defrosted and puréed in a blender or food processor until smooth

If you are planning to serve the French toast immediately, preheat the oven to 400°F, with the rack in the center position. If you are doing this in advance (up to 12 hours), stop just before baking the filled "sandwiches." Select a heavy baking sheet large enough to hold 6 French toast "sandwiches" in one layer. Line it with foil to make for easy cleanup.

This recipe can be assembled, up to the final baking, the night before and refrigerated on a baking sheet covered in plastic wrap or aluminum foil. Or it can be frozen for up to 3 months, wrapped in plastic wrap, and thawed for 45 minutes before baking.

To make the French toast: Add the eggs, milk, and vanilla to a pie pan or shallow bowl and whisk to combine. Use a flat metal spatula to dip the slices of bread, first one side and then the other, quickly in the mixture just to moisten them but not long enough for them to fall apart. Place each of the slices on the foil-lined baking sheet as you dip them. Heat 1 tablespoon of the butter in a large skillet set over moderate heat. When the butter sizzles, add the slices of bread, several at a time, and cook until the undersides are golden brown. Flip the bread and cook on the other side until golden brown. Repeat with the remaining butter and bread slices, removing them to the baking sheet as they finish cooking.

Make the filling by whisking together the softened cream cheese, sugar, orange zest, and liqueur or orange juice in a small mixing bowl until smooth. Place approximately 2 tablespoons of the filling on each of 6 slices of bread, spreading it slightly but not to the edges with the back of a spoon. Top each slice with a second slice and press down with your hand or a metal spatula to seal them together. If you will be serving the French toast later, wrap the baking sheet airtight in plastic wrap and refrigerate for up to 12 hours. Allow the bread to come to room temperature before placing the baking sheet in the oven.

To bake the French toast: Have the oven preheated to 400°F. Place the baking sheet in the oven and cook for 15 to 20 minutes, or just until the insides are hot. You can tell this by inserting the tip of a small, sharp knife into a "sandwich" and then feeling it to see whether it's hot.

Serve the "sandwiches" on heated plates with a generous drizzle of strawberry sauce.

2 appetizers

All our married life, my husband has made fun of my quest to see the Green Flash. He's as convinced that I am making this up as I am convinced that if I keep looking I will see it. For those who believe in it (that would be someone like me), the Green Flash is the elusive green burst of light that sometimes happens at the horizon over a cloudless sea just as the sun sinks out of sight.

"Elusive" is the operative word here, since this phenomenon seems to happen in places where I am not. I've gazed at sunsets over every ocean from the Atlantic to the Indian and from practically every continent and have yet to see it— but that doesn't stop me from trying. Summer evenings I position myself on our deck to watch the sun sink over Cape Cod Bay in hopes that this might be the night. The nonbelievers on hand, coached by my husband, voice their skepticism. I've learned that the only way to keep the hecklers quiet is to offer them a drink with alcohol and something to eat. Perhaps this is how the first appetizer was invented. I often share the story of my quest to see the Green Flash with people I meet while watching the sunset from Herring Cove Beach in Provincetown. Recently I met a woman who had not only once seen the Green Flash, but had encountered something even better. One bitterly cold winter day just before sunset she saw a pod of right whales surfacing close to shore. They were blowing (as in "Thar she blows!"), and the spray from their blowholes as well as the water splashed up by their enormous tails turned to ice crystals in the frigid air. The setting sun pierced those frosty waterfalls and made rainbows dance over the water.

Vacation days offer the luxury of extra time to enjoy leisurely meals comprising more than one course. While many of us could eat a whole meal made of appetizers (hence the Spanish tradition of tapas, or small meals), the idea of beginning dinner with an appetizer course elevates the dining experience to a new level of enjoyment. Whether you serve tidbits with drinks before coming to the table or a plated course, taking the edge off ravenous hunger stoked by a day at the beach or in the garden puts you and your family or guests in an instantly good mood. Just think how good my mood would be if I could stand on my deck, freshly shucked oyster in hand, and see, just for once, the magical Green Flash.

Baked Stuffed Clams

Serves 4 as an appetizer

While some folks consider this dish an appetizer, my family can make a whole meal of it. I imagine it started out as a way to stretch a single mollusk into something more filling by adding breadcrumbs. There are recipes that call for additions like ground sausage and all sorts of fancy herbs, but I think they just take away from the flavor of the clams. If you shuck your own clams, finding shells to stuff won't be a problem. If you buy your clams already shucked, be sure to ask for shells to stuff them back into.

3   tablespoons mild olive oil

1   medium onion, peeled and finely diced

2   cloves garlic, peeled and minced

¼   cup fresh flat-leaf (Italian) parsley, leaves only, chopped

1   cup toasted breadcrumbs (see box)

6   tablespoons unsalted butter, at room temperature

2   dozen hard-shell clams, shucked and chopped, shells and liquid reserved (page 55)

Salt and freshly ground black pepper

Tabasco sauce

Lemon wedges

Preheat the broiler to high with the rack in the upper third of the oven. Heat the olive oil in a medium-sized skillet set over moderate heat. Add the onion and cook, stirring frequently, until it is wilted and golden. Add the garlic and cook for another 4 to 5 minutes without allowing the garlic to brown. Place the onion, garlic, and any pan drippings in a medium-sized bowl. Stir in the parsley and breadcrumbs. Add the soft butter and, using a fork or your fingers, blend the ingredients together to form a soft paste. Mix in the clams and their liquid. Add salt, pepper, and Tabasco sauce to taste. If the mixture is too soft to hold together, add a bit more of the breadcrumbs. Distribute the stuffing among the clamshells, pressing down lightly with your fingers to secure it. Place the clams on a heavy-duty baking sheet and broil for 5 minutes, or until the stuffing is golden brown. Serve hot with lemon wedges.

To toast breadcrumbs, arrange them in a shallow layer on a heavy-duty baking sheet and bake them at 300°F for 10 to 12 minutes, until lightly browned. Cool on the pan before placing in an airtight container. They will keep for up to 6 months in the freezer.

Irma's Clam Fritters

Serves 4 to 6 as an appetizer

Of all the treasures I've found on Cape Cod, none is as precious as the friendship of Jessica Baron, who started out as my veterinarian and almost immediately became a friend. When Jessica introduced me to her aunt Mary Frankel, I knew I had found a soul mate, and an enduring friendship began. It seemed inevitable that Mary's wonderful daughter Joanna and my son Max would meet and fall in love. Knowing Jessica has enriched and grown our family in ways that we are thankful for every day.

Jessica's mother, Irma, was revered for many reasons, but her ability to make clam fritters is the first thing I heard about, and after I tasted her recipe (made by Mary one lovely September evening), I could see why.

This recipe can be made with freshly steamed clams or minced clams available in many markets and fish stores. Minced clams should be quickly cooked in their juice and enough water to cover, at a gentle simmer, for 3 to 4 minutes. Drain before cooking and reserve the liquid for the recipe.

2   cups all-purpose flour

2   teaspoons baking powder

1   teaspoon salt

$\frac{1}{2}$ teaspoon freshly ground black pepper

1   medium onion, peeled and chopped

1   egg, beaten

1   to 1$\frac{1}{2}$ cups clam juice

1$\frac{1}{2}$ cups minced clams

    Vegetable oil for frying

    Tartar Sauce (page 197)

In a medium-sized mixing bowl, whisk together the flour, baking powder, salt, and pepper. With a wooden spoon, mix in the onion, stirring until it is coated. Stir in the egg and clam juice, adding more if necessary to make a batter the consistency of pancake batter. Add the clams and stir to coat them with the batter.

Heat 2 inches of vegetable oil in a large skillet set over high heat until a drop of water added to it sizzles immediately. Line 2 baking sheets with paper towels. Use a tablespoon to drop walnut-sized balls of batter into the oil, cooking only 4 to 5 at a time. Crowding the pan affects the cooking temperature and makes for soggy fritters. Cook until brown, 3 to 4 minutes, turning once halfway through the cooking time to brown the top side. Cut into the first of the fritters to make sure it is cooked through. Use a slotted spoon to place the cooked fritters on the paper towel–lined baking sheets. Serve immediately with tartar sauce.

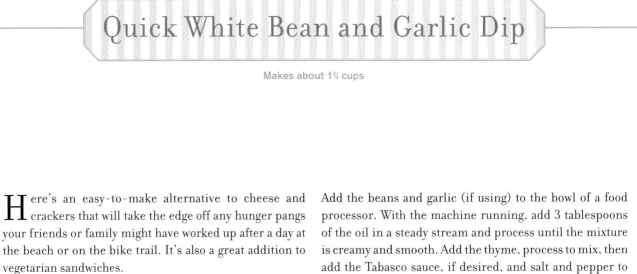 Quick White Bean and Garlic Dip

Makes about 1¾ cups

Here's an easy-to-make alternative to cheese and crackers that will take the edge off any hunger pangs your friends or family might have worked up after a day at the beach or on the bike trail. It's also a great addition to vegetarian sandwiches.

1   16-ounce can white beans, drained

4   tablespoons garlic oil (available in supermarkets and specialty food stores), or 4 tablespoons olive oil and 2 large cloves garlic, peeled

1   teaspoon fresh thyme, leaves only

2   drops Tabasco sauce (optional)

     Salt and freshly ground black pepper

Add the beans and garlic (if using) to the bowl of a food processor. With the machine running, add 3 tablespoons of the oil in a steady stream and process until the mixture is creamy and smooth. Add the thyme, process to mix, then add the Tabasco sauce, if desired, and salt and pepper to taste. Spoon and scrape the mixture into a small serving bowl or ramekin, cover, and refrigerate for up to 3 days before serving.

To serve, drizzle with 1 tablespoon of oil and pass with sliced crusty bread, wedges of pita bread, chips, or vegetable sticks.

Classic Deviled Eggs

Makes 12 eggs

Deviled eggs were once so popular that you could buy dedicated serving platters boasting a dozen shallow, yolk-colored indentations that prevented your eggs from sliding around while your guests passed the plate. I don't own a deviled egg platter, but that doesn't stop me from making our special Cape Cod version of this dish. People who remember deviled eggs from the days when they made an appearance at any picnic or cocktail party worth attending will be delighted to be reacquainted with them, and those who've never had the pleasure will welcome the introduction.

6   extra-large eggs

1   tablespoon white vinegar

2   teaspoons Dijon mustard

4   to 5 drops Tabasco sauce

2   teaspoons anchovy paste

       Salt and freshly ground black pepper

¼   cup mayonnaise

1   tablespoon snipped fresh chives

12   smoked oysters or smoked mussels (page 60)

Place the eggs in a 1½-quart saucepan and cover with cold water. Add the vinegar. Place the pan, uncovered, over medium-high heat and bring to a full boil. Reduce the heat to a simmer, and cook for 15 minutes. Drain and plunge the eggs into ice water; allow to chill completely before peeling. Refrigerate until cool, and then use a sharp knife to slice the eggs in half lengthwise. Carefully scoop out yolks, place them in a bowl, and mash with a fork. Add the mustard, Tabasco sauce, anchovy paste, and salt and pepper to taste. Stir in the mayonnaise and chives.

Use a small spoon or a pastry bag fitted with a star tip to fill each egg white with about 2 teaspoons of the egg yolk mixture. Top each with a smoked oyster or mussel. Refrigerate until ready to serve.

Fried Clams

Serves 4 to 6 as an appetizer

You'll need whole soft-shell clams (steamers) to make this recipe. Like many of the clam and oyster recipes in this book, this one gives you the option of doing the shucking or buying them already shucked from your fishmonger. If you dig your own clams, you might want to take the step of purging them of sand. (See box for directions.)

The very best version of these is made my friend Joe Polombo, who insists that his trick of using Japanese breadcrumbs (Panko—the kind used to make tempura dishes) yields the crispiest clams. If you have a Japanese grocery near you, you might want to try it, but otherwise bread or cracker crumbs give a quite nice result. The temperature of the frying oil is also key, so be sure to use a thermometer. If the oil is too cool, the breading absorbs it and becomes soggy; if the oil is too hot, the clams will burn before they are cooked through.

1   cup all-purpose flour

1   teaspoon salt

½   teaspoon freshly ground black pepper

2   eggs, lightly beaten

2   tablespoons whole milk or cream

1   cup breadcrumbs, cornmeal, or cracker crumbs (such as oyster crackers)

3   to 4 cups vegetable oil for frying

40   steamers, cleaned and shucked

     Tartar Sauce (page 197) for serving

     Lemon wedges for serving

Line several baking sheets with a double layer of paper towels. Line another baking sheet with waxed paper or plastic wrap. Place the flour in a shallow bowl and stir in the salt and pepper with a fork. Mix the eggs and cream together in a second shallow bowl. Place the crumbs in a third shallow bowl. Pour 3 cups of the oil into a heavy sauté pan set over medium-high heat. Dip the clams, one at a time, into the flour to coat well. Dip them next into the egg mixture and finally into the crumbs to coat completely. Set the coated clams on the waxed paper or plastic-lined baking sheet.

When the oil registers 375°F, use a slotted spoon to carefully slip no more than 6 clams at a time into the hot oil—if you crowd the pan, the cooking temperature will be reduced and the clams will get soggy. Cook for 1½ minutes, then use the slotted spoon to turn them over and cook for another 1½ minutes—only until they are golden brown. Immediately remove to the paper towel–lined baking sheet. Repeat with the other clams, adding more oil if necessary, and serve them as soon as humanly possible, with tartar sauce and a squeeze of fresh lemon juice.

To clean soft-shell clams (steamers), rinse the shells under cold running water, then soak them for several hours (or overnight) in a bucket of sea (or salt) water to which you have added a few handfuls of cornmeal. This will remove sand or grit in the clams. Refrigerate the clams during this process. Rinse again before shucking.

Raw Bar

I imagine that if you're a fan of raw shellfish you've wondered who had the nerve to eat that first raw oyster. Someone desperately hungry, you'd have to guess. Thank goodness someone took the bold step so that the rest of us could jump right in and indulge away. Yes, raw oysters, clams, and other shellfish are an acquired taste, but once you've made the leap you will either be totally seduced or continue to wonder what the big fuss is about.

Serving oysters on the half shell by themselves, or along with cherrystone or littleneck clams, makes a dramatic beginning to a meal, be it a barbecue or New Year's Eve feast. Adding some simple boiled shrimp and perhaps some smoked mussels (recipes follow) will give your less adventurous guests something to eat while others concentrate on the uncooked items.

World-famous Cape Cod Wellfleet oysters are sweet and briny at the same time—if you close your eyes while you eat one you can't help thinking of the sea.

The local hard-shell clams (quahogs) that are good for eating raw come in two sizes. My taste runs to the very smallest, which are called littlenecks. They measure about $1^1/_2$ to $2^1/_4$ inches across. The next size up are cherrystones, which are around $2^1/_4$ to 3 inches across. Like the oysters, they have a sweet, briny taste, but with a chewier consistency.

When selecting shellfish (whether it is to be served raw or cooked), it is absolutely essential to know and trust your source and to make sure it is regulated by an agency that monitors the purity of the water from which the shellfish was harvested. The results of consuming a bad or contaminated oyster or clam can be debilitating at best and deadly at worst.

I usually figure on a combination of 6 clams and/or oysters per person.

Shellfish should be refrigerated until you shuck them, which you should do no more than a few hours before eating. First, they need to be thoroughly scrubbed. I use a steel brush and lots of cold running water.

Shuck clams in the sink or over a shallow tray, first slipping the hand you'll use to hold the shell into a sturdy rubber or heavy cloth glove. Place the clam in the palm of your open hand. Slip the tip of a clam knife between the two shells (this is a little tricky and takes some practice). Once you wedge the tip in, hold the clam tight and turn it to get the point of the knife as close as possible to the muscle that holds the shells together. Twist the knife (or the clam) to open the hinge, and remove and discard the top shell. Run the knife under the clam to detach it from the bottom shell, allowing it to remain in the shell for serving. Chances are that someone will be standing nearby, ready to eat the clam. If not, place it on a tray in the refrigerator while you shuck the rest.

Shucking oysters is a little more of a challenge, but it's a skill that anyone with a little patience (and lots of oysters on hand) can master. Protect the oyster-holding hand with a sturdy glove. Slip the point of an oyster knife (or clam knife) or a "church key" can opener between the shells near the hinge, wiggling it back and forth to loosen the muscle. As the shells begin to move apart, move the knife or church key further in until the top shell opens. Remove it and then slide the knife (not the church key) under the oyster to detach it from the shell. Leave the oyster in the bottom shell for serving.

Clam and oyster shells are notoriously tippy and don't behave well when placed flat on a serving plate. Since you don't want to lose any of the liquid, there are several ways to make them stay put. Some people make a bed of rock or coarse salt (about $1/2$ to 1 inch deep) and make little indentations in which to rest the shells. Another way is to line the dish with seaweed (which your fishmonger can get with enough notice) and nestle the shells in it. If the weather is very warm and the shellfish might be sitting out for more than 15 minutes, I usually rest them on a layer of crushed ice sprinkled with coarse or kosher salt. The salt lowers the melting point of the ice.

Being of the "less is more" school, I like my oysters and clams with only a squirt of fresh lemon juice. Anything else (such as cocktail sauce) instantly masks the flavor. However, if your shellfish cry out for cocktail sauce, use the recipe on page 197.

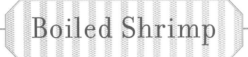

Boiled Shrimp

Serves 6 as an appetizer

Boiled shrimp are a traditional part of any raw bar, probably to satisfy people who aren't interested in eating raw shellfish. Although you can buy bags of frozen, shelled, and deveined shrimp in the supermarket, the taste and texture of fresh shrimp cooked in the shell can't be beat. If you do use frozen shrimp, follow the cooking instructions below, and do not defrost them before cooking.

1½ pounds extra-large or large shrimp, fresh or frozen (26 to 30 count or 31 to 35 count)

6 cups water

2 tablespoons pickling spices (available in the spice section of the supermarket)

Cocktail Sauce (page 197; optional)

If you are using fresh shrimp, place them in a colander and rinse well with cold water. If the heads are on the shrimp, twist them off, then shell the shrimp by pulling off the legs, and then slipping off the shell. Use a small, sharp knife to cut a shallow slit down the top side of the shrimp, and hold the slit open under cold running water to flush out the dark vein. You may also need to pull it out with your fingers. If you are squeamish about this procedure, you have the option of performing it after the shrimp are cooked or of asking someone else to do it.

Place the water in a large saucepan, add the pickling spices, cover, and bring to a rapid boil. Add the shrimp, cover the pot, and cook for 5 minutes, or just until all the shrimp have turned pink. If you are using frozen shrimp, add them to the boiling water as is. Overcooking will make the shrimp tough. Empty the pot into the colander and immediately run cold water over the shrimp until they are cold. Rinse off the pickling spices and refrigerate the shrimp in a covered container or reclosable plastic bag until ready to serve. Serve with the cocktail sauce, if desired.

Scallop Seviche

Serves 6 as an appetizer

There was a time (before sushi became popular) when most Americans wouldn't dream of eating raw fish. Back then, both Europeans and South Americans were enjoying the delicate flavor and freshness of both fish and shellfish "cured" briefly in lemon and lime juices. The beauty of this elegant appetizer with its straight-from-the-ocean taste is that it takes a very few minutes to prepare and can be made ahead of time.

Although this recipe calls for scallops, you can certainly add or substitute any mild white fish, such as striped bass, flounder, sole, or cod.

It should go without saying that this must be made with absolutely fresh shellfish and/or fish that has not been previously frozen.

1½ pounds scallops (bay or sea), muscle removed (see box), cleaned and patted dry

1 teaspoon chile paste, or 1 serrano or 2 jalapeño chiles

1 small cucumber, unwaxed if possible

Juice of 1 large lemon (reserve the peel for garnish)

Juice of 3 limes

¼ teaspoon mild Asian sesame oil

1 tablespoon soy sauce

⅓ cup fresh cilantro leaves, torn into quarters (tearing rather than chopping avoids giving the leaves a bitter, soapy taste)

1 tablespoon peeled and finely minced fresh ginger

12 cherry tomatoes, quartered

½ cup finely minced red onion

Sea salt and freshly ground black pepper

Long strips of finely julienned lemon zest for garnish

Making long, thin strips of lemon peel is a bit time-consuming, but it's the perfect job for someone who asks the cook, "How can I help?" Supply him or her with a cutting board, a small, sharp knife, and somewhere to sit down. Instruct your helper to slice off the ends of the lemon so it can sit upright. Then use the knife to cut away the rind in wide strips from one end to the other. Flip the rind over so that the white pith is exposed, and then slide the knife down between the pith and zest to remove as much pith as possible. Finally, use a heavy chef's knife to cut the strips lengthwise into very thin strips. Your guest will either love this job or never volunteer for anything again.

⊹⟩ ⟨⊹

The tough muscle that looks like a flap attached to the scallop is what holds the scallop shell together. The larger the scallop, the larger the muscle will be. If you want to add some flavor to fish stock or make a nice base for soup or chowder, add the removed muscles to a pan containing ½ cup white wine, ½ cup water, and a few tablespoons fresh herbs of your choice. Simmer for 15 minutes and strain.

Cut the scallops across the grain into $\frac{1}{4}$-inch-thick slices. If you are using bay scallops and they are very small, leave them whole. If using chiles rather than chile paste, cut them in half, remove the seeds, and then cut into very fine julienne. (Wear rubber gloves to protect your hands from the volatile oil.) Peel the cucumber if it is waxed, quarter it lengthwise, and slice it paper-thin.

Place the scallops in a nonreactive (preferably glass or ceramic) mixing bowl. Add the lemon and lime juices, sesame oil, soy sauce, cilantro, ginger, and chile paste or chiles to a second mixing bowl and toss to combine. Add the tomatoes, cucumber, and onion, tossing to combine. Finally, fold in the scallops, season with salt and pepper to taste, cover the bowl with plastic wrap, pushing the wrap down so that it touches the surface of the mixture, and refrigerate for at least 6 hours but not more than 12, as the scallops will start to get mushy.

A very elegant (and trendy) way to serve seviche is in martini glasses. Of course, serving it on a simple plate is equally acceptable. Garnish with the lemon zest.

Smoked Mussels

Serves 6 as an appetizer

I own a stovetop smoker and find it's the easiest way to smoke anything from shellfish to meat, poultry, and vegetables. It's also quite straightforward to smoke food in an outdoor grill (see the instructions below).

3   pounds mussels, shells scrubbed and fibrous "beards" pulled off (see box)

¼   cup golden mustard

¼   cup (packed) dark brown sugar

2   tablespoons soy sauce

To smoke the mussels in a stovetop smoker: Line the smoker with foil and wood chips according to the manufacturer's directions. Position the rack and add the mussels. Slide the lid closed and place the smoker over moderate heat. Cook for 20 to 30 minutes, or until the mussels have opened. Discard any that do not open.

In a small bowl, mix together the mustard, brown sugar, and soy sauce. Remove the mussels from their shells, toss them in the sauce, and place them in a disposable foil pan. Place the pan into the smoker. Cover and cook over moderate heat for 15 minutes. Chill well before serving.

To smoke the mussels in a covered grill: Soak 2 cups of wood chips in water for 30 minutes. Add the mussels to a shallow disposable aluminum pan. Light a gas or charcoal grill. When the coals are white-hot, drain the wood chips and scatter them directly on the coals, or place them in a small disposable aluminum pan and place the pan directly on the coals. Position the rack and place the pan containing the mussels on it. Cover the grill and cook until the mussels open. Remove the mussels, discarding any that have not opened.

In a small bowl, mix together the mustard, brown sugar, and soy sauce. Remove the mussels from their shells, toss them in the sauce, return them to the foil pan, and place it back on the grill. Cover the grill and cook for another 15 minutes, adding more wood chips if you placed the first chips directly on the coals, or to get a smokier flavor. Chill before serving.

Leftover mussels can be mixed with a little mayonnaise and lemon juice to make a snack, salad, or cold appetizer.

The fibrous threads that you'll find at the hinge end of the mussel shell are called the beard. This is what the mussel uses to attach itself to the rocks from which it grows. After scrubbing the shells with a stiff brush, hold the mussel under cold running water and firmly grasp the shell in one hand and the threads, close to the shell, between your thumb and forefinger. Give an assertive yank to pull them out as close to the meat as possible. This should be done before the mussel is cooked.

Smoked Salmon Cheesecake

Makes one 9-inch cheesecake, to serve 12 to 14

When I created this recipe and Craig Claiborne ran it in the *New York Times Magazine,* it was just about the most exciting moment of my life. This cheesecake remains one of my favorite appetizers and the one I think of instantly when I have to feed a crowd. Perfect for a buffet or sliced and set upon a bed of greens, it makes a very filling start to a meal and should be followed by a light main course.

The key to success here is to make sure the cream cheese is at room temperature and that you use a food processor, not a mixer, to make the filling. A mixer incorporates air into the batter, which makes the cake rise during baking and then sink during cooling. While not a fatal flaw, this is certainly a cosmetic imperfection.

Look for lox bits (the ends left over after the whole smoked salmon is hand sliced) at your local deli. You will save a lot of money.

For the crust

½   cup fine French breadcrumbs, lightly toasted

¼   cup finely grated Gruyère cheese

2   teaspoons dried herbes de Provence (see box)

For the filling

3   tablespoons unsalted butter

1   medium onion, peeled and minced

½   cup finely diced red bell pepper

½   cup finely diced green bell pepper

1¾   pounds (28 ounces) regular cream cheese (not whipped, low-fat, or nonfat), at room temperature

4   extra-large eggs

⅓   cup heavy cream

½   cup grated Gruyère cheese

1   scant teaspoon salt

½   teaspoon freshly ground black pepper

3   or 4 drops Tabasco sauce

8   ounces smoked salmon, cut into ½-inch pieces

⅓   cup grated Parmesan cheese (Reggiano preferred)

62

Preheat the oven to 300°F, with the rack in the center position.

Select a 9-inch springform pan, 3 inches deep. Wrap the outside bottom and sides with heavy-duty foil, pressing it tight to secure it against the sides of the pan. Generously coat the bottom and sides of the pan with 1 tablespoon of the butter. I like to add a circle of parchment on the bottom and butter that, too, just to make the cheesecake really easy to get out of the pan.

To make the crust: In a small mixing bowl, toss the breadcrumbs together with the cheese and herbs and sprinkle over the bottom and sides of the pan, tilting the pan to cover as much of the sides as possible. Allow any loose crumbs to fall back into the bottom of the pan.

To make the filling: In a skillet set over medium heat, melt 2 tablespoons of the butter and sauté the onion, stirring occasionally, until soft and translucent. Add both bell peppers and cook, stirring occasionally, for 4 to 5 minutes, or until soft.

Place the cream cheese, eggs, and heavy cream in the work bowl of a food processor fitted with the metal blade. Process, scraping down the sides as necessary to incorporate all the ingredients, until absolutely smooth. Add the Gruyère, salt, pepper, and Tabasco sauce, processing until just mixed. Add the sautéed vegetables and pulse just to

> **Herbes de Provence,** a mixture of dried herbs from the south of France, can be found in many gourmet specialty stores, or you can make your own by combining equal amounts of dried thyme, basil, sage, rosemary, chervil, tarragon, and lavender. Store in a tightly sealed glass jar in a cool, dark place. Make only a small amount at a time, as it loses its potency if stored for very long.
>
> This cheesecake freezes fairly well. The consistency will change a bit, but not enough to make a huge difference.

combine, then add the smoked salmon and pulse just to mix. Try not to overmix the batter; it shouldn't be a smooth purée. Pour and scrape the batter into the prepared pan, smoothing the top with a rubber spatula. Sprinkle with the grated Parmesan.

To bake the cheesecake: Place the springform pan in a roasting pan large enough so that the sides of the pans don't touch. Place the pan in the oven and then add enough hot water to come halfway up the sides of the springform pan—not over the top of the foil.

Bake for 90 minutes, checking every 30 minutes to add more hot water if necessary. If, toward the end of the baking time, the top is getting too brown, cover it loosely with foil. At the end of the baking time, turn off the oven and allow the cheesecake to remain inside for 1 hour before removing it to a wire rack to cool completely.

Remove the sides of the springform pan, place a light tray or wire rack on top of the cheesecake, and flip it over to remove the bottom and parchment, if used. Invert the cake right-side up and serve by cutting it in very thin wedges with a long, thin, sharp knife that has been dipped in hot water and wiped dry.

This is best served at room temperature.

3 soups and chowders

"Manhattan or New England?" is never a choice on Cape Cod. We think the idea of putting tomatoes into clam chowder and making the soup thin and watery is worse than ludicrous—it's a travesty. While we feel sorry for folks who cross the bridge looking for the "wrong stuff," we know that once they have it our way, there is no going back.

Chowder should coat a spoon, stick to your ribs, and make you happy all over. Ideally you should be sitting at a picnic bench, the sun on your back, your feet in sandals, and the afternoon full of endless possibilities stretched out in front of you—all the way to sunset on the beach. A pat of melting butter and a sprinkle of paprika decorates the surface of your chowder. Cubes of soft (but never mushy) potato melt in your mouth. Tender nuggets of sweet clams offer just the mildest resistance to your teeth, golden bits of sautéed onion and freshly ground black pepper accent the brew. The base makes you think of warm cream, and while you eat you are already wondering if you can justify another helping.

 Kale Soup

Serves 8

"Of course you're going to have a recipe for kale soup," said Peter Cook, our Dune Tour driver, as we careened up and over yet another impossibly high hill of sand. The tires of the '76 Chevy Suburban, with Art's Dune Tours written across the door, were intentionally soft, and the truck was in four-wheel drive. Since Peter had been doing this for many, many years, we simply relaxed and enjoyed the spectacular view. The sun slunk low over the acres of bleached sea grass, turning the wind-whorled peaks and valleys of constantly shifting sand to ten shades of gold. We watched a hooded seal float on his back while he lazily munched on a small skate, with seagulls circling overhead screaming for him to share his meal.

Peter told us stories of old Provincetown, pointing out the lethal shoals where more than 3,000 ships had foundered. He pointed across the water toward the Azores, home to his family before they sailed across to Cape Cod.

"Make sure you get an authentic Portuguese recipe," he advised me as the van turned back onto the blacktop highway, "and don't forget the chorizo!"

Chorizo and linguiça are spicy pork sausages that are staples in Portuguese, Spanish, and Mexican cuisine. You can find them in many supermarkets (often frozen, which is fine), ethnic markets, and by mail order from companies that advertise online. If you can't find it, you can substitute the pork sausage of your choice. You can also make your soup with spicy chicken or turkey sausage, if you wish.

8	ounces dried white pea beans, small limas, or chickpeas (see box)
¼	cup olive oil
1	large onion, peeled and diced
2	large cloves garlic, peeled and diced
8	cups beef stock
10	ounces chorizo or linguiça sausage, thinly sliced
4	Idaho potatoes, peeled and cut into ½-inch cubes
8	cups finely julienned kale, stems trimmed before cutting

Salt and freshly ground black pepper

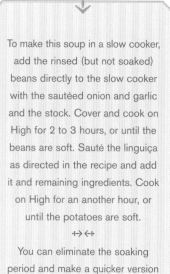

To make this soup in a slow cooker, add the rinsed (but not soaked) beans directly to the slow cooker with the sautéed onion and garlic and the stock. Cover and cook on High for 2 to 3 hours, or until the beans are soft. Sauté the linguiça as directed in the recipe and add it and remaining ingredients. Cook on High for an another hour, or until the potatoes are soft.

↦ ↤

You can eliminate the soaking period and make a quicker version of this soup by starting with canned beans. Drain them well, rinse with cold water, and begin the recipe where you are instructed to sauté the onion and garlic.

Soak the beans, at room temperature, in twice their volume of cold water overnight. Drain and add to a large pot.

Heat the oil in a large sauté pan set over moderate heat and cook the onion, stirring frequently, until it is golden. Lower the heat and add the garlic and cook for an additional 5 minutes, stirring frequently, taking care not to let the garlic burn. Add the onion and stock to the beans, cover, and cook at a low simmer for 45 minutes, or until the beans are soft but not mushy. Add the chorizo or linguiça to the sauté pan. Cook over moderate heat for 10 minutes, stirring frequently, until the sausage has given up some of its fat. Use a slotted spoon to transfer the sausage to the pot, and discard the fat. Add the potatoes and kale. Cover, bring the mixture back to a simmer, and cook for 15 to 20 minutes, or until the potatoes are soft. Add salt and pepper to taste and serve hot along with a loaf of crusty bread for dipping.

Ginger Pumpkin Bisque

Serves 8

A velvet firecracker is what someone once called this smooth-as-silk soup with a bit of a bite. You can make it with fresh or canned pumpkin and serve it hot or cold.

1   3-by-1-inch-piece fresh ginger, peeled and minced

    Finely grated zest of 1 large orange

3   large carrots, peeled and cut into 1-inch slices

2   pounds sweet potatoes, peeled and cut into 2-inch cubes

2   10-ounce cans pumpkin purée, or 2½ cups fresh pumpkin purée (see page 72)

1   large Spanish onion, peeled and diced

6   cups chicken or vegetable stock

1   cup orange juice

    Salt and freshly ground black pepper

3   to 4 drops Tabasco sauce

    Sour cream or plain yogurt for garnish

    Toasted pumpkin seeds (see box) for garnish

Place the ginger, orange zest, carrots, sweet potatoes, pumpkin, onion, stock, and orange juice in a large, covered, heavy-bottomed nonreactive stockpot set over moderate heat. Simmer until the vegetables are very tender—about 30 minutes. Cool for 30 minutes before puréeing the soup, either in a blender or with a hand-held blender. Add salt, pepper, and Tabasco sauce to taste. Garnish each bowlful with a dollop of sour cream or plain yogurt and top with toasted pumpkin seeds just before serving.

continued

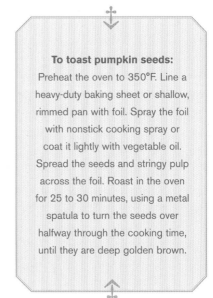

To toast pumpkin seeds:

Preheat the oven to 350°F. Line a heavy-duty baking sheet or shallow, rimmed pan with foil. Spray the foil with nonstick cooking spray or coat it lightly with vegetable oil. Spread the seeds and stringy pulp across the foil. Roast in the oven for 25 to 30 minutes, using a metal spatula to turn the seeds over halfway through the cooking time, until they are deep golden brown.

⚓

To prepare fresh pumpkin purée: Select a sugar pumpkin (the kind with the variegated vertical stripes). Scrub the surface, cut off the stem, cut the pumpkin in half, and remove the seeds and stringy pulp. Use a sharp knife to remove the outer skin. Cut the flesh into 2-inch chunks and place them in a large, heavy-bottomed pot. Add water to cover and set over high heat until the water comes to a simmer. Lower the heat, cover the pot, and simmer gently until the pumpkin is very tender—about 20 minutes. Drain before using.

You can also make pumpkin purée in the oven. Preheat the oven to 350°F, with the rack in the lower third of the oven but not the lowest position. Scrub the outside of the pumpkin and slice off the stem. Cut the pumpkin in half and scoop out the seeds and pulp. Save the seeds for toasting, if you like. Place the pieces, cut-side down, in a foil-lined roasting pan. Use a fork or the tip of a small knife to cover the surface of the pumpkin with shallow holes every few inches. Pour about 1 inch of water into the bottom of the pan and bake the pumpkin until very soft, 40 to 60 minutes. Cool until you can handle the pumpkin. Turn the pieces over and scoop out the flesh, discarding the outer skin.

This is the perfect recipe to make in either a slow cooker or pressure cooker. It will take about 4 hours on High in the slow cooker or 12 to 15 minutes in the pressure cooker.

↦ ↤

Slow cookers and pressure cookers are invaluable kitchen tools, especially when it comes to soup. I often add a medley of vegetables and some vegetable broth to the slow cooker in the morning, cook them on Low for most of the day, and then use my immersion (stick) blender to purée the mixture just before we sit down to dinner. The next day that lovely soup, thickened without cream or a roux, is served cold.

P. J.'s Fish Chowder

Serves 4

My very dear friend P. J. Hamel's husband, Rick, is an Orvis fishing guide. One summer day at dusk, I watched him fly-cast off the rocks of Pamet Harbor in Wellfleet. Guys who had been surf-casting with 8-foot rods and reels the size of cable spools winked and nudged each other as Rick (complete with vest and waders) stepped onto the jetty, shaded his eyes, and looked out over the smooth bay waters for a moment before, with ballet grace and exquisite precision, placing his fly in the exact spot he had chosen. Seconds later, a 3-foot striped bass was thrashing at the end of his silken line. The guys on the beach shut up pretty quickly (seeing as their plastic coolers were empty except for bait).

While you can make P. J.'s splendid fish chowder with just about any fillets you choose, if you do happen to have some fresh striper on hand, by all means go for it.

5   tablespoons butter

1   large or 2 medium onions, peeled and coarsely chopped

2   large Idaho potatoes, peeled and diced into ½-inch pieces

    About 1½ cups water or Quick Fish Stock (page 206)

1   to 1½ pounds boned fish fillet, such as cod, striped bass, halibut, hake, cusk, flounder, or other plain white fish, cut into 2-inch pieces

3   cups light cream or evaporated milk

    Salt and freshly ground white pepper

1   teaspoon dried thyme, or 1 tablespoon fresh thyme leaves

    Paprika for garnish

Melt 4 tablespoons of the the butter in a 3-quart saucepan set over moderate heat. Add the chopped onions and sauté until they are golden but not brown. Put the diced potatoes atop the onions, and add water or fish stock just to cover. Then lay the fish atop the potatoes.

Bring the liquid to a boil and simmer just until the potatoes are cooked through, 10 to 15 minutes; the fish will be cooked (via steam) at this point, too. Use a fork to stir the soup, flaking the fish.

Add the cream, and stir gently to blend. Season with salt and white pepper to taste, and add the thyme. Heat just to a simmer, but don't actually let the soup boil. Turn off the heat and let it sit for 10 minutes or so to let the flavors blend. Serve hot, with the remaining butter and a sprinkling of paprika on top.

Clam Chowder

Serves 8 generously

Here on Cape Cod there are as many recipes for clam chowder as there are clams in the sea. This one takes the very best elements of several dozen versions and puts them together to make a creamy, rich meal in a bowl that even New Yorkers will have to admit beats anything with tomatoes.

Although you can certainly start by digging and shucking your own clams, most fish stores and many supermarkets sell shucked, chopped clams—my preference. While some recipes call for thickening clam chowder with flour, I don't like the library paste texture that can result (actually, I don't like to use any thickener at all), so those of you who are used to the thick consistency of many commercial varieties will find this soup on the thin side. If you wish to thicken it up, see the instructions at the end of the recipe.

3 ounces salt pork or thick slab bacon, diced

1 large yellow onion, peeled and chopped into medium dice

3 stalks celery (with leaves), rinsed and cut into small dice

3 cups Idaho potatoes, peeled and cut into ¼-inch cubes

4 cups bottled clam juice

1½ pints (3 cups) chopped fresh clams, drained, liquid reserved

2 cups whole milk

4 cups light cream

Salt and lots of freshly ground pepper

½ cup (1 stick) butter, cut into slices, for garnish

Paprika for garnish

continued on next page

Place the salt pork or bacon in a heavy skillet and set over moderate heat. Cook, stirring occasionally, until the meat is brown and crisp; then use a slotted spoon to remove it to a paper towel to drain. Add the onion and celery to the drippings and cook over moderate heat, stirring frequently, until they are wilted and the onion is golden. Use the slotted spoon to add the cooked salt pork or bacon and vegetables to a soup kettle. Discard the fat in the sauté pan and scrape any of the brown drippings that remain into the soup kettle. Add the potatoes and clam juice (both the bottled juice and the liquid reserved from the fresh clams). Set the kettle over high heat, cover, and bring to a rapid simmer, then reduce the heat and cook for 15 to 20 minutes, or until the potatoes are tender. Stir in the milk and cream and heat, uncovered, without allowing the mixture to boil. When the mixture is hot, add the clams and cook for another 5 minutes without boiling. Season with salt and pepper to taste. Serve immediately, ladling the chowder into heated bowls and garnishing each with a pat of butter and a sprinkling of paprika.

For a thicker chowder, add 3 tablespoons all-purpose flour to the pan after you have cooked and removed the salt pork and drained off all but 3 tablespoons of the fat. Whisk continuously over moderate heat until the mixture is smooth. Cook 5 minutes, stirring constantly. Add this slurry to the chowder after the potatoes have been cooked, and stir well to combine. Simmer over moderate heat, stirring constantly, until the chowder is slightly thickened before adding the remaining ingredients.

Oyster Stew

Serves 4

This magnificently simple yet wildly indulgent dish is my idea of a close-to-perfect meal. If you are handy at opening oysters, start with them in the shell. If you're in a hurry and are lucky enough to have a fishmonger who is willing to do all the work, buy the oysters shucked. Either way, make sure you save, or ask for, the liquid from the shells. Have your heated soup bowls ready before you start.

- 4 cups light cream
- ½ cup bottled clam juice or Quick Fish Stock (page 206)
- 32 fresh oysters, shucked (see pages 54–55), liquid reserved
- ½ cup (1 stick) unsalted butter
- 1 tablespoon Worcestershire sauce

  Salt and freshly ground white pepper

  Paprika for garnish

Place the cream, clam juice or stock, and reserved oyster liquid in a 2- to 3-quart pot set over medium heat and, stirring frequently, heat to just below a simmer. Cover and keep hot on low heat. In a large, heavy-bottomed sauté pan, melt the butter over medium heat and cook the oysters, turning once or twice and shaking the pan to move them around, just until the edges begin to curl, 5 to 6 minutes. Add the oysters and butter to the hot cream, add the Worcestershire sauce, season with salt and pepper to taste, and ladle into hot bowls. Garnish with a sprinkling of paprika and serve immediately, passing a dish of oyster crackers.

Saffron-Scented Cod and Tomato Soup

Serves 4

Every fall the town of Truro has a week called Truro Treasures, which is a celebration of life in this special place (and perhaps an opportunity to reclaim the land after the tourists have left for the season). Truro has one treasure that exists year-round: the Atlantic Spice House, located on Route 6 just where 6A splits off, becoming a two-lane, sand-dusted ribbon lined with beach cottages boasting the world's best front yard.

From the outside it would be hard to guess that the huge gray warehouse holds a treasure trove of hard-to-find spices and herbs along with teas and coffees from every corner of the earth. Dried fruits of every description are nestled in large barrels next to cinnamon sticks and tiny sachets for making your own potpourri. Herbes de Provence redolent with lavender, thyme, and rosemary perfume the air with an aroma that makes you think you've taken a trip to someplace wonderfully exotic without having to get on a plane.

Store manager Linnet Hultin not only sells to restaurants far and wide but also has a brisk mail-order business. So if you can't drive to Truro for your saffron (although it's worth a trip), you can call her at 800-316-7965 to place an order or receive a catalog. She generously shared this recipe for a marvelously colorful and equally flavorful fish soup that is garnished with a slice of toasted French bread and a dab of aïoli (garlic mayonnaise).

¼ cup mild olive oil

1 medium onion, peeled and minced

3 cloves garlic, peeled and minced

3 cups fish or vegetable stock

1 14-ounce can stewed tomatoes and their juice, coarsely chopped

2 tablespoons balsamic vinegar

1 tablespoon tomato paste

2 bay leaves

1 tablespoon fresh thyme leaves, or 1 teaspoon dried thyme

¼ teaspoon crushed red pepper flakes

⅛ teaspoon dried saffron threads (about 20 threads)

1 pound cod fillets, cut into 1-inch chunks

Salt and freshly ground black pepper

4 ½-inch slices Italian or French bread, toasted

Aïoli (page 80)

Freshly grated Parmesan cheese

continued

Heat the oil in a large, nonreactive soup pot over medium heat. Cook the onion, stirring frequently, for 4 to 5 minutes, or until softened. Add the garlic and cook for 1 to 2 minutes more, being careful not to burn the garlic. Add the stock, tomatoes, vinegar, tomato paste, bay leaves, thyme, red pepper flakes, and saffron. Bring to a boil, reduce the heat, and simmer, uncovered, stirring occasionally, for 15 minutes. Add the cod and stir gently to combine. Cover, and adjust the heat so that the fish simmers gently for 5 to 7 minutes, or until it is just cooked through but not falling apart. Taste for seasoning and add salt and pepper to taste. Remove the bay leaves before serving.

To serve, ladle the soup into heated bowls. Float a slice of toast on top of each serving, then spoon a generous dollop of aïoli on each slice. Pass the grated Parmesan separately.

Toasting saffron before you use it brings out even more flavor. The easiest way to do this is on a piece of foil in a toaster oven set at 300°F for 5 minutes.

Aïoli

Makes about 1½ cups

This garlicky mayonnaise is a classic garnish for hearty fish soups.

- 1 large whole egg
- 1 large egg yolk
- 2 large cloves garlic, peeled and coarsely chopped
- 1 teaspoon Dijon mustard
- ½ cup mild olive oil
- ½ cup extra-virgin olive oil
- 1 tablespoon strained fresh lemon juice

   Salt and freshly ground black pepper

Place the whole egg and the yolk in the work bowl of a food processor fitted with the metal blade. Process until well blended, about 15 seconds. Add the garlic and mustard and process for 10 seconds. Combine the oils in a spouted measuring cup. With the motor running, pour about 1 tablespoon of oil into the feed tube of the processor. When that has been incorporated into the egg mixture, add another tablespoon of oil to the feed tube. Add 4 more tablespoons in the same manner, and then pour the remaining oil into the tube. When all the oil is incorporated, the aïoli should be thick and light. Add the lemon juice and process until combined. Scrape the aïoli into a bowl and season with salt and pepper to taste.

Use immediately, or store in a covered container in the refrigerator for up to 2 days.

Bread Bowl Salmon Chowder

Serves 6

Have your soup and eat the bowl as well is the theory behind this innovative dish that seems to be hugely popular with children, who love the concept of eating the dish along with the meal. With the proliferation of artisanal bakeries, finding boules—the round rolls that are perfect for this dish—is easier than ever.

- 6 round, domed loaves of bread, 6 to 8 inches in diameter
- 3 tablespoons butter
- 4 shallots, peeled and minced
- 1 teaspoon dried tarragon
- 4 medium red-skinned potatoes, unpeeled, thinly sliced
- 1/2 teaspoon salt
- 1/8 teaspoon freshly ground white pepper
- 2 teaspoons Worcestershire sauce
- 2 cups Quick Fish Stock (page 206) or purchased fish stock
- 1 1/2 pounds salmon steaks, 3/4 to 1 inch thick
- 1 lemon, thinly sliced
- 1 bay leaf
- 1 cup dry white wine
- 1 cup (1/2 pint) heavy cream
- 6 slices bacon, cooked until crisp and broken into small pieces for garnish

Use a serrated knife to slice off the top third of each loaf of bread. Use your fingers to scoop out the interior to form a bowl. Save the crumbs for another use.

In a large skillet set over medium heat, melt the butter; add the shallots and cook, stirring, until soft but not browned. Add the tarragon, potatoes, salt, pepper, Worcestershire sauce, and fish stock. Reduce the heat, cover the pan, and simmer gently for 15 minutes.

Add the salmon steaks in a single layer; cover with lemon slices, then add the bay leaf. Pour in the wine. Cover again and cook over low heat until the salmon flakes when tested with a fork and the potatoes are tender, 10 to 12 minutes. Remove and discard the bay leaf and lemon slices. Remove the salmon steaks; pick out the bones, remove the skin, and cut the salmon into 1 1/2-inch chunks. Add the cream to the liquid in the pan and cook over medium heat until the mixture simmers. Cook for 5 minutes, then gently mix in the salmon. Taste and add salt if needed. Place the bread bowls in rimmed dishes or large bowls, spoon the chowder into the bread bowls, garnish with the bacon, and serve immediately.

Portuguese rolls, available in bakeries on the Cape and in neighborhoods that specialize in Portuguese foods, make a great bowl for this chowder. Since they are soft, it's important to toast them in a 350°F oven for about 12 minutes, after slicing off the tops and scooping out some of the interior.

vegetables and salads

More often than not, mealtime finds at least one vegetarian at our table, so in addition to whatever else I'm serving I try to make sure there is at least one hearty dish that would satisfy someone of that persuasion. Starting a meal with a salad or even making a whole meal of a salad is something that is done more and more often these days.

Farm stands that offer organic locally grown fruit and produce dot every road on the Cape, so there is never an excuse not to have seasonal vegetables from early summer right through Thanksgiving. We have tender lettuce and early squash in June, sweet corn, tomatoes, and basil in midsummer, and potatoes and pumpkins as well as the famous Eastham (or Truro, depending on where you live) turnips in the fall. Each one of these vegetables is heavenly all by itself or served in concert with the others.

Dried Cranberry, Walnut, and Blue Cheese Salad

Serves 6

Almost every upscale restaurant on the Cape serves a version of this salad. You can modify or change the ingredients to suit your own taste, using raisins in place of dried cranberries, pecans in place of walnuts, and field greens or red-leaf lettuce instead of spinach. The one thing I wouldn't change is the blue cheese, which gives the salad its signature creamy and assertive texture and flavor. You may wish to use another kind of blue cheese, such as Stilton or even Gorgonzola. The counterpoint of the dried fruit and blue cheese is heavenly.

For the dressing

3   tablespoons apple cider vinegar

1   shallot, peeled and minced

½   cup vegetable oil

Coarse sea salt and freshly ground black pepper

For the salad

¼   cup dried cranberries

¼   cup walnut pieces

2   green apples, cored and cut into ¼-inch cubes

4   ounces Maytag blue cheese, crumbled

1   pound baby spinach, rinsed and well dried

To make the dressing: Combine the vinegar and shallot in a medium-sized mixing bowl. Whisk in the oil in a slow, steady stream until it is completely incorporated and the mixture is slightly thickened. Season with salt and pepper to taste.

To assemble the salad: Add the cranberries, walnuts, and apples to the bowl with the dressing and toss to coat. Add the blue cheese and mix gently so that the cheese remains in discrete pieces. Distribute the spinach among 6 salad plates and top with the cranberry mixture.

Cape Cod Turnips

Serves 8

Cape Cod turnips aren't really turnips at all, according to Donna Foley, who sells locally grown fruits and vegetables at the Crow Farm stand in Sandwich. They are actually Macomber rutabagas—more like daikon radish in consistency than traditional turnips (which can be substituted in this recipe). Also called Eastham or Truro turnips, they are large, heavy, pale orbs sporting tall greens that can be blanched and served as a side vegetable.

Donna told me that her favorite uses for Cape Cod turnips are in New England Boiled Dinner (page 106) and as a substitute for mashed potatoes. My family raved about the mashed turnips, and I thought they were pretty swell myself—sort of like a lighter mashed potato. They would be great with that Thanksgiving turkey.

Even though the giant turnips are seductive, try to select smaller or medium-sized ones, as the larger ones can be woody inside. The easiest way to peel them is to slice enough off both ends so that the turnip rests squarely on the work surface. Using a sharp, heavy chef's knife held almost parallel to the turnip, slice off the skin, leaving as much of the root as possible. This takes some practice, but it's much easier in the long run than using a peeler. If, when you cut the turnip open, you do find woody, brown fiber, just cut it off and discard it.

3   to 4 pounds Cape Cod turnips (or regular turnips), outer peel removed, cut into 1½-inch cubes

2   teaspoons salt, plus more to taste

½   cup (1 stick) butter

Freshly ground black pepper

Place the turnips in a large pot and add water to cover. Add the 2 teaspoons salt, cover the pan, and bring the mixture to a rapid boil over high heat. Reduce the heat to medium and simmer until the turnips are very tender when pierced with a fork, 12 to 15 minutes. Drain off the water, add the butter, and mash with a potato masher. Add salt and pepper to taste and serve hot.

This can be made up to a day ahead and refrigerated in a covered container. Microwave to reheat.

Cape Corn and Rice Salad

Serves 6 to 8

Even though the very best corn on the cob is cooked soon after being picked, there are plenty of uses for days-old corn. The following salad is one of my favorites. The trick of simmering the corncobs to make a cooking liquid for the rice imparts a lovely sweetness to the finished dish.

6   ears sweet corn, husks removed, ears simmered in boiling water to cover for 5 minutes, drained and cooled

2½ cups milk (whole, low-fat, or nonfat)

1   cup long-grain rice (not instant or quick cooking)

1   large red bell pepper, cut in half, seeded, cored, and cut into ½-inch dice

1   pint cherry tomatoes, halved

1   small red onion, peeled and diced

½   cup fresh basil leaves, shredded (see box)

½   cup mayonnaise

¼   cup balsamic vinegar

¼   cup soy sauce

Hold the cooked corn on end, stem-side down, on a cutting board. Run a sharp knife down the sides to remove the kernels. Place the kernels in a large mixing bowl, cover the bowl with plastic wrap, and leave at room temperature while you prepare the rice.

Place the corncobs and milk in a skillet set over medium heat. Cover the pan, bring the mixture to a low simmer, and cook, covered, for 10 minutes. Discard the cobs and measure the liquid. Add more milk, if necessary, to measure 2½ cups. Add the rice to the milk, cover, and simmer for 15 to 20 minutes, or until the rice is cooked and the milk is absorbed. Check the rice occasionally and add milk or water if it dries out. Fluff the cooked rice with a fork and allow it to cool to room temperature.

Add the rice to the bowl with the corn. Stir in the bell pepper, tomatoes, onion, and basil. In a small bowl, whisk together the mayonnaise, vinegar, and soy sauce. Pour the mayonnaise mixture over the salad and stir to mix well.

To shred basil: Roll the leaves into narrow cylinders, and then cut them into narrow ribbons with a sharp knife.

Cauliflower Flans

Serves 6 as a first course

My first real experience working in a restaurant was at a five-star French landmark Cape Cod establishment where the sous-chef alternately made my life miserable and taught me almost everything I know about putting a finished dish on the table. As a boss, Bob Kinkead was a breathtakingly tough and unforgiving taskmaster; as a chef there are few who can touch his talent and creative genius. As a restaurateur and businessman, he sets the standard when it comes to knowing how to do it—and how to give back to the business. As a friend (which, thank God, he turned out to be), there are none as loyal, supportive, and affirming. Next time you are in Washington, D.C., run, don't walk, to eat at Kinkead's—and tell 'em Lora sent you.

This elegant and super-flavorful flan will make you look at cauliflower with a new respect.

1	small head cauliflower, cut into florets (about 2 cups)
1	cup (½ pint) heavy cream
1	cup milk
2	cloves garlic, peeled
1	teaspoon salt
½	teaspoon freshly ground white pepper
2	large eggs
1	large egg yolk
¼	cup freshly grated Reggiano Parmesan

Combine the cauliflower, cream, milk, garlic, salt, and pepper in a 1½-quart nonreactive pan set over medium-high heat. Bring to a low simmer and cook, uncovered, for 15 to 20 minutes, until the cauliflower is very tender. Remove from the heat and cool to room temperature. Add the cooled mixture to a blender or food processor. Add the eggs, egg yolk, and Parmesan and purée until smooth.

Preheat the oven to 300°F, with the rack in the center position. Spray six 4-ounce ramekins with nonstick cooking spray. Fill the molds four-fifths full, and place them in a shallow roasting pan or on a heavy-duty rimmed baking sheet. Place the pan in the oven before adding enough hot water to come halfway up the sides of the cups or ramekins. Bake for 35 to 45 minutes, or until a toothpick inserted in the center of the flan comes out clean.

To serve, invert the mold and release the flan. If serving as a first course, place on a plate with lightly dressed greens, or serve as a side vegetable on a dinner plate.

Caramelized Onion Mashed Potatoes

Serves 6

The sugar content in "sweet" onions such as Vidalia, Maui, Texas 10-15's, and Walla Walla is what sets them apart from your "garden variety" onion. This sugar turns to deep golden brown as the onions slowly cook. The caramelizing is what gives these mashed potatoes their heavenly taste. Caramelized onions can be made up to a week ahead of time.

For the onions

½   cup (1 stick) butter

2   large Vidalia or other sweet onions, peeled and cut into 1-inch slices

For the potatoes

6   Idaho potatoes, peeled and cut into 2-inch pieces
    Salt and freshly ground black pepper

To make the caramelized onions: Heat the butter in a sauté pan set over moderate heat. Add the onions and stir with a wooden spoon to coat. Turn the heat to low and simmer the onions, stirring occasionally, until they are deep brown. This will take at least an hour and perhaps longer. Take care not to let the onions burn. An alternative technique is to place the onions and butter in a slow cooker, cover, and cook on High for 24 hours, or until the onions are deep brown.

Drain the liquid from the onions and reserve it in a covered container in the refrigerator, where the butter will rise to the top and solidify. If you are making the mashed potatoes immediately, do not refrigerate the onions.

To make the potatoes: Bring a large pot of salted water to a rapid boil over high heat. Add the potatoes and cook, uncovered, until they are quite tender—15 to 20 minutes. Drain off the cooking liquid, leaving the potatoes in the pot. Add the caramelized onions, the butter from the top of the reserved liquid, and ½ cup of the onion liquid. Use a potato masher to mash the potatoes to the desired consistency (I like mine on the slightly lumpy side), adding additional onion liquid if necessary. Season with salt and pepper to taste, and serve hot.

Mac's Calamari Salad

Serves 6 as an appetizer, 4 as a main course

Mac's Seafood in Wellfleet offers things most other seafood stores do not. First, right out the back door is the beach and a wraparound view of Wellfleet Harbor, with its fleet of fishing and pleasure boats rocking gently on sparkling blue water. Next is the selection of fresh-from-the-ocean fish and shellfish that makes it hard to decide what to cook for dinner. There's the house-smoked bluefish, salmon, scallops, and whatever else Mac feels like putting in his smoker that day. Of course, there is also the sushi bar, where you can stand and watch a decidedly non-Japanese but wonderfully talented young man roll fresh lobster in rice and wasabi-spread nori to make—yes, you guessed it—lobster sushi. The people who work behind the counter, always ready to share their vast knowledge of how to cook whatever is in the case, are a bonus for those who can't decide between broiled, grilled, baked, fried, or raw. If all this isn't enough, there's the promise of a fantastic ice cream sundae if you walk around to the front of the building, where it's hard to make yet another selection . . . let's see, will it be pistachio or maple walnut . . . rocky road or fudge ripple?

Mac's calamari is sold out almost as soon as it hits the case. When you taste it, you'll understand why. Making this the night before and letting it sit in the refrigerator allows the flavors to meld and blend.

- 1 cup white wine
- 1 cup water
- 1 pound squid, cleaned and cut into ¼-inch rings
- ¼ cup vegetable oil
- 2 tablespoons lemon juice
- 2 tablespoons lime juice
- ½ cup diced celery
- ¼ cup cilantro leaves, torn into pieces
- 1 clove garlic, peeled and minced
- 1 medium red bell pepper, cut in half, seeded, cored, and cut into small dice
- 1 medium green bell pepper, cut in half, seeded, cored, and cut into small dice
- 2 small jalapeño peppers, cut in half, seeds removed, and finely chopped
- 3 medium cucumbers, peeled and diced
- 3 scallions, white and green parts, ends trimmed and thinly sliced

Salt and freshly ground black pepper

Combine the wine and water in a sauté pan set over moderate heat. Bring to a simmer, add the squid, and simmer for 2 minutes. Immediately drain the squid and rinse with cold water to stop the cooking.

Add the oil, lemon and lime juices, celery, cilantro, garlic, peppers, cucumber, and scallions to a large bowl. Mix to combine. Stir in the squid. Cover the bowl with plastic wrap and refrigerate for at least 6 hours or for as long as 24 hours. Stir, add salt and pepper to taste, and serve over greens.

Roasted Potatoes

Serves 6

S erve these with steak, chicken, or a hearty fish preparation, or for breakfast instead of home fries.

18   to 24 small Red Bliss potatoes, scrubbed

1   large Spanish onion, peeled and cut into
     1/4-inch dice

1   tablespoon fresh thyme leaves, or 1 teaspoon
     dried thyme

1   teaspoon kosher salt, or to taste
     Freshly ground black pepper

1/2 cup mild olive oil

4   large cloves garlic, peeled and thinly sliced

Preheat the oven to 450°F, with the rack in the center position. Cut the potatoes into quarters and use paper towels to dry them very well. This is important, or they won't be crispy. Place the potatoes and onion in a large mixing bowl. Add the thyme, salt, and pepper to taste and toss to combine. Add the oil to an ovenproof baking dish, and place it in the oven for 10 to 15 minutes, or until the oil sizzles. Add the potatoes and onion to the hot pan (carefully, since the oil may splatter), toss to coat, and roast for 30 minutes, stirring every 10 minutes. Sprinkle the garlic on top, stir to combine, and roast for an additional 10 minutes. The potatoes should be deep golden brown and the garlic a golden brown. If you plan to serve this for breakfast, you can prepare it completely the day before, cool, and refrigerate in the roasting pan (covered with foil). Drizzle with a few more tablespoons of olive oil before reheating, uncovered, in a 400°F oven for about 15 minutes.

Roasted Asparagus

Serves 6

Asparagus loves sandy soil, and Cape Cod offers a perfect place to cultivate it. Over the years, however, the crops dwindled, and now the only place you can find asparagus on the Cape is in home vegetable gardens. You can occasionally still find it growing wild by the roadside.

This recipe can be made well ahead and refrigerated for several days before serving.

2½ pounds fresh asparagus of uniform size, woody ends trimmed, rinsed and patted dry

½ to ⅔ cup mild olive oil

Coarse sea salt and freshly ground black pepper

¼ cup balsamic vinegar

Preheat the oven to 425°F, with the rack in the upper third of the oven but not the highest position. Line a heavy-duty rimmed baking sheet or roasting pan with foil (this helps with cleanup). Place the asparagus in one layer on the foil and drizzle the oil over it. Turn the stalks to coat them with oil. Sprinkle with salt and pepper. Roast the asparagus for 15 minutes, then use tongs to turn the stalks over and roast for another 5 to 8 minutes, until the underside browns. The stalks should be quite brown and crisp. Remove the pan from the oven, drizzle with the vinegar, and allow the asparagus to cool to room temperature. If you plan to serve this within 6 hours, cover and let it rest at room temperature; otherwise, remove it to a clean container, adding any liquid left in the pan, cover, and refrigerate until ready to serve.

To choose asparagus, look for unwilted, plump stems with firm, closed heads. Avoid stalks with vertical lines, which indicate dryness, or mushy tips, which mean the vegetable is past its prime.

Sunset Slaw

Serves 8

This slightly unorthodox recipe for coleslaw got its name when we served it at a beach picnic one summer evening. Someone pointed out that the colors of the sunset and the colors of the coleslaw were almost the same.

I came up with this recipe as a way to justify my addiction to those tiny pickled onions found in the bottom of a martini. I can live without martinis—it's the onions I crave, and since I never know when I'll need to whip up some of this coleslaw, it makes sense to keep a few jars on hand, right?

For the salad

1   cup pickled beets, drained, with juice reserved

1   small red cabbage, stem-end trimmed, core removed, and outer leaves peeled, about 1½ pounds or 3 cups

1   cup pickled cocktail onions, the smaller the better, a few tablespoons of juice reserved

For the dressing

½   cup prepared mayonnaise, regular or low-fat, or to taste

¼   cup (firmly packed) dark brown sugar

¼   cup reserved beet juice

2   to 3 tablespoons reserved onion juice

2   tablespoons soy sauce

1   tablespoon caraway seeds

Shred the beets and the cabbage, either by hand or using the shredding disk of a food processor. If the onions are larger than marbles, slice them in half.

In a large salad bowl or other container, whisk together the mayonnaise, brown sugar, beet and onion juices, and soy sauce. If the dressing is too astringent for your taste, add a few more tablespoons of mayonnaise. Stir in the caraway seeds. Add the cabbage, beets, and onions and toss well to combine. Chill for at least 1 hour before serving.

Two Salmon and Potato Salad

Serves 8 to 10

Wild-caught Atlantic salmon is a whole different animal from its bland, farm-raised distant cousin. If you haven't had the pleasure of tasting the difference, make it a point to do so the next time you have the chance. The smoked salmon in this recipe gives a whole new depth of flavor as well as a sublime richness to the texture. This recipe for not-your-everyday potato salad was created by my wonderful friend Barbara Lauterbach, who, although she spends most of her time up north in New Hampshire, loves Cape Cod almost as much as I do.

For the dressing

¼ cup balsamic vinegar

½ cup extra-virgin olive oil

1 tablespoon Dijon mustard

¼ cup chopped fresh dill

4 scallions, white and green parts, thinly sliced

2 tablespoons soy sauce

Freshly ground black pepper

For the salad

2 pounds Red Bliss or red new potatoes

1 cup shelled green peas

1½ pounds Poached Salmon (recipe follows), flaked

½ pound smoked salmon, cut into 1½-inch pieces

½ cup sliced radishes

4 hard-boiled eggs, quartered

Lettuce leaves for serving

To make the dressing: Add the vinegar and oil to a small bowl. Whisk to make an emulsion. Add the mustard, dill, scallions, soy sauce, and pepper to taste, and whisk to blend.

To make the salad: If the potatoes are very small, leave them whole; otherwise, cut them in half. Add them to a pot of rapidly boiling salted water and cook over medium-high heat until fork-tender. Drain and cool. Peel if desired.

Bring a saucepan three-fourths full of water to a boil. Add the peas and boil just until tender, between 2 and 4 minutes, depending on the size.

Drain and immediately place the peas under cold running water to set the color. Drain well.

In a large serving bowl, combine the potatoes, both kinds of salmon, peas, radish slices, and eggs. Add the dressing and toss gently. If not serving immediately, cover and chill.

To serve, line a large serving platter with the lettuce leaves. Spoon the salad onto the lettuce leaves. Serve at once.

Poached Salmon

Makes 1½ pounds

1½ pounds salmon steaks

¼   teaspoon dried tarragon, or 1 teaspoon fresh tarragon leaves

¼   teaspoon dried thyme, or 1 teaspoon fresh thyme leaves

4   or 5 sprigs flat-leaf (Italian) parsley

1   bay leaf

4   or 5 whole black peppercorns

¾   cup dry white wine

¾   cup water

1   teaspoon salt

Select a nonreactive pan large enough to hold the fish in one layer. Cut a piece of parchment to fit the diameter of the pan, and coat one side generously with butter. Set aside. Cut a piece of cheesecloth to measure 5 by 5 inches, and place the herbs, bay leaf, and peppercorns on it. Gather the corners and use kitchen twine to tie them securely to form a small packet. This is called a bouquet garni.

Add the bouquet garni, wine, water, and salt to the pan. Set over high heat and bring the mixture to a boil. Reduce the heat so the liquid simmers. Cover and simmer for 10 minutes. Remove the bouquet garni. Add the salmon steaks and additional water to cover, if necessary. Top with the prepared parchment and cook at a bare simmer for 10 to 12 minutes, or just until the salmon flakes when tested with a fork. Use a wide spatula to remove the salmon from the liquid, and refrigerate until it is cool enough to handle. Remove and discard the skin and bones, and flake the salmon with a fork.

5 main courses

"W hat's for dinner?" is a very important question, and it's even more important when you live in or are visiting a place with as much potential for great food as Cape Cod. The amazing wealth of indigenous ingredients, from lobster to cranberries, sparks the imagination and ignites the desire to have every meal showcase the Cape's bounty. From the simplest of fish preparations that can be made quickly on the grill to dishes that perfume the kitchen through long hours of simmering on the back of the stove, the opportunities to celebrate the flavors of Cape Cod make for sublime main courses.

Grilled Pork with Cran-Asian Sauce

Serves 6

I was asking my friend Mark Leighton the wine maven about cranberry liqueurs. He directed my attention to cranberry wine made by Plymouth Colony Winery and offered his own recipe for using it in a marinade shot through with Asian ingredients. The combination of sweet and pungent works marvelously well here—and Mark suggests drinking some of the cranberry wine, well chilled, along with the dish.

For the marinade

1   cup cranberry wine, or ¾ cup cranberry juice and ¼ cup dry sherry

¼   cup soy sauce

1   tablespoon black bean sauce (available in Asian groceries)

2   tablespoons Asian sesame oil

6   cloves garlic, peeled and minced

1   tablespoon ginger, peeled and minced

1   small onion, peeled and minced

2   tablespoons catsup

2   tablespoons balsamic vinegar

Strained juice of 1 lemon

2   tablespoons honey

1   tablespoon mild chile oil

For the pork

3   pounds boneless pork, cut into 2-inch strips

½   cup chopped fresh cilantro leaves for garnish

½   cup dried cranberries for garnish

To make the marinade: Combine the marinade ingredients in a deep bowl. Remove 1 cup of the marinade and reserve it to finish the pork after grilling.

To marinate and grill the pork: Add the pork strips to the marinade in the bowl, mixing to coat both sides. Cover with plastic wrap and refrigerate overnight.

Light a charcoal or gas grill, or preheat the broiler to medium-high, with the rack in the upper third of the oven. Grill or broil the pork for 8 to 10 minutes on each side, or until the center is no longer pink. Remove the meat to a heated platter, spoon the reserved marinade on top, and garnish with chopped cilantro and a sprinkling of dried cranberries.

Grilled Flank Steak

Serves 5 to 6

This easy-to-cook, wonderful-tasting cut of meat is often overlooked by folks with an eye toward steak on the grill. Usually less expensive than the more popular rib-eye and porterhouse steaks, thin slices of marinated, grilled flank steak were made to marry a side of Caramelized Onion Mashed Potatoes (page 91).

It's sometimes a challenge to find a large flank steak, so using two is fine, especially when you consider that you might have leftovers and how good cold flank steak sandwiches are.

- ¼ cup soy sauce
- ¼ cup Dijon mustard
- 3 tablespoons red wine vinegar
- 1 cup mild olive oil
- 2 tablespoons molasses
- 3 cloves garlic, peeled and smashed with the side of a knife
- 1 medium onion, peeled and coarsely diced
- 1 2½- to 3-pound flank steak, or 2 smaller steaks

Combine the soy sauce, mustard, vinegar, oil, molasses, garlic, and onion in a freezer-strength reclosable plastic bag or a shallow pan and shake (after sealing the plastic bag) or whisk to combine. Place the steak or steaks on a cutting board and use a sharp knife to cut crosshatches, ½ inch deep, every 2 inches on the surface of both sides. Add the steak to the plastic bag and seal, or add it to the pan, cover with plastic wrap, and refrigerate for at least 2 hours or as long as 12 hours.

Light a grill, or preheat a broiler, with the rack set in the upper third of the oven. Remove the steak from the marinade, reserving a little of the liquid to baste the steak during cooking. Grill or broil for 5 to 6 minutes per side for rare, 7 to 8 minutes per side for medium. Baste 2 or 3 times during the cooking process. Allow the steak to rest for 5 minutes before using a long, thin knife to slice it on the diagonal into ½-inch pieces.

New England Boiled Dinner

Serves 6

The idea of walking into a cozy home and having the seductive aroma of something wonderful to eat is what this recipe is all about. An Irish friend of mine told me that her grandmother, who worked as a housekeeper to rich Bostonians, told her that New England boiled dinner appeared every Thursday night on the menus of restaurants throughout Boston. The reason was that Thursday was the help's night off, and corned beef was their dish of choice.

This is one of my family's very favorite cold-weather meals, and I like to think of it as the dish that keeps on giving. Leftovers have the potential to appear in all sorts of other dishes. If you've never had the pleasure of a cold brisket sandwich, I suggest saving some of the leftovers for this purpose.

It's important to buy first-cut or flat-cut corned beef, which means the meat has been trimmed of most of the fat before you buy it.

You can substitute an additional can of beef broth in place of the stout or beer, if you wish.

3	pounds first-cut or flat-cut corned beef
2	14½-ounce cans low-sodium beef broth
1	cup Guinness Stout or other dark beer
3	tablespoons Dijon mustard
⅔	cup (packed) dark brown sugar
2	tablespoons molasses
1	tablespoon dried dill

2	bay leaves
3	whole cloves and 6 black peppercorns, tied in cheesecloth
3	large Idaho potatoes, peeled and cut into ½-inch slices
4	carrots, peeled and cut into ½-inch slices
1	small head green cabbage, outer leaves discarded, cut into 8 wedges, core removed
16	small white onions, peeled and left whole, or one 10-ounce bag frozen pearl onions, not defrosted
2	parsnips, peeled and cut into ½-inch slices

Place the corned beef in a large, heavy-bottomed soup kettle or in a large (5½- to 6-quart) slow cooker. Add the broth, stout or beer, mustard, brown sugar, molasses, and dill to a small mixing bowl and whisk to combine. Pour the mixture over the meat. Tuck the bay leaves and spices tied in cheesecloth into the side of the pot, under the surface of the liquid.

Cover and bring to a low simmer on the stovetop. Cook for 3 hours, or until the meat is very tender.

Remove the meat from the pot, skim off any fat, and add the vegetables. Cover, bring to a simmer, and cook for about 20 minutes, or until the vegetables are tender. Slice the meat against the grain and serve with the vegetables and a little of the cooking liquid. Discard the bay leaves before serving.

Roasted Chicken with Oyster Cracker Stuffing

Serves 4 to 5

Oyster crackers aren't just for chowder. They make a tasty stuffing as well. You can buy oyster crackers in most supermarkets and fish stores. I try to find a capon (a large roasting chicken) to make this. If the chickens you find are smaller (broilers), you can make two using the same amount of stuffing, dividing it between the two birds.

1   large (5-pound) roasting chicken, or two broilers (2½ pounds each), whole

5   tablespoons butter, 1 tablespoon melted

1   cup diced onion, plus 1 medium onion, peeled and sliced

1   cup diced celery

1   tablespoon fresh rosemary leaves, or 1 teaspoon dried rosemary

1⅔ cups chicken stock

3   cups oyster crackers

½   teaspoon freshly ground black pepper, plus more to taste

    Salt

Preheat the oven to 375°F, with the rack in the center position. Butter or spray a baking pan with nonstick cooking spray. Remove the giblets from the inside of the chicken, reserving the neck. Rinse the cavity and dry it with paper towels. Melt 4 tablespoons of the butter in a large skillet set over moderate heat, and sauté the diced onion and celery until golden brown. In a large bowl, combine the cooked onion and celery and their cooking juices, the rosemary, ⅔ cup of the stock, the oyster crackers, and the ½ teaspoon pepper. Stir to completely coat the crackers with the liquid. Let the stuffing rest for 5 to 7 minutes to allow the crackers to absorb some of the liquid.

Place three-fourths of the stuffing in the large cavity of the bird, mounding it slightly at the opening. Tie the legs together with kitchen twine to keep the stuffing in place. Place the remaining stuffing in the neck cavity, then pull the flap of skin down over it. Insert a meat thermometer deep into the thigh (but not so deep that it touches a bone), and place the chicken breast-side up in the baking pan. Brush the exposed areas with the 1 tablespoon melted butter and sprinkle with salt and pepper. Scatter the sliced onion in the pan around the bird, then pour in the remaining 1 cup chicken stock. Roast the chicken for 2 to 2½ hours, or until the thermometer reads 185°F, and the juices run clear when the thigh is pierced with the tip of a sharp knife.

Immediately spoon the stuffing into a warmed serving dish, carve the chicken, and serve hot.

Chicken Pot Pie

Makes 6 individual pies

There used to be the most wonderful place for lunch in West Barnstable called Ojala Farm. Run by sisters who, I believe, were Norwegian, it was in a tiny, white-painted, slightly ramshackle roadside building with a front porch and a line of eager diners that snaked out from the door, across the porch, and into the tree-shaded front yard. The menu was small, but we didn't care—just as long as we could be assured of getting one of those chicken pot pies. Like many wonderful things, Ojala Farm is closed. But the building remains. Every time I pass, I hope that somewhere there is a Norwegian relative looking for a place to open a restaurant.

You can make your own pie crust from scratch or use the store-bought frozen kind (which seems to be quite decent). You can also substitute cooked turkey or even raw oysters for the chicken in this recipe.

For the crust

2½	cups all-purpose flour
1½	teaspoons salt
1	rounded tablespoon granulated sugar
5	tablespoons unsalted butter, cut into ½-inch pieces and chilled or frozen
½	cup solid vegetable shortening, chilled
1	extra-large egg
1	extra-large egg yolk
2	tablespoons white vinegar
3	to 4 tablespoons ice water

For the filling

3	tablespoons butter
4	scallions, white and green parts, root-end trimmed, cut into ¼-inch slices
2	cups sliced white mushrooms
¼	cup all-purpose flour
3	cups chicken or turkey stock
3	cups cooked chicken or turkey, cut into large dice (about 1½ inches)
1½	cups frozen peas, slightly defrosted
1½	cups frozen pearl onions, slightly defrosted
½	teaspoon dried sage
½	teaspoon dried rosemary
1	scant teaspoon salt
½	teaspoon freshly ground black pepper

For the egg glaze

¼	cup milk or cream
1	extra-large egg yolk, lightly beaten

To make the crust: Sift the flour, salt, and sugar into a mixing bowl. Scatter the pieces of butter and shortening over the top and use 2 butter knives in a crisscross motion or a pastry blender to cut the fat into the flour until it resembles coarse, uneven crumbs. Combine the egg, egg yolk, vinegar, and 3 tablespoons of the ice water in a 2-cup measure or other spouted pitcher. Dribble in the liquid while you use a fork to stir the flour mixture, adding more liquid if necessary to form a dough that just begins to hold together. Turn the dough and any leftover dry ingredients in the bowl out onto a very lightly floured work surface. Use your flour-dusted hands and a dough scraper to quickly knead the dough into a ball. Cut the ball into 2 equal pieces, and flatten it slightly. Wrap each piece airtight in plastic wrap and refrigerate for at least 1 hour.

Working with one piece at a time (leaving the other in the refrigerator), roll the dough out on a lightly floured work surface until it is about $\frac{1}{8}$ inch thick. Using an individual pie tin or a 2- to 3-cup ramekin or casserole dish as a guide, cut 6 circles (or ovals) of dough, 1 inch larger than the tin or casserole. Use a wide metal spatula to transfer the pieces of dough to a baking sheet, and refrigerate until ready to assemble the pie.

To make the filling: Melt the butter in a medium saucepan set over moderate heat. Add the scallions and mushrooms and cook, stirring frequently, until the vegetables have wilted and the mushrooms have begun to weep, about 5 minutes. Sprinkle the flour over them and stir constantly for 3 minutes, or until the flour is absorbed. Slowly add the stock while you stir or whisk the mixture. Bring the mixture to a simmer and cook for 2 minutes, stirring or

whisking constantly. Add the chicken, peas, onions, herbs, salt and pepper. Remove from the heat. This filling can be refrigerated for up to 2 days.

To assemble the pies: Preheat the oven to 400°F, with the rack in the lower third of the oven but not the lowest position. Select a heavy-duty baking sheet large enough to hold all 6 pie tins, ramekins, or casseroles. You might want to line the baking sheet with foil to make for easy cleanup.

Lightly butter 6 individual pie tins or 2- to 3-cup ramekins or ovenproof casserole dishes. Butter 1 inch of the outside edge as well. Divide the filling among the prepared containers, filling them right up to the top. Depending on the size, you might have some filling left over. Lay one of the prepared pie crusts on top of each, sealing the sides by molding the dough to the outside rim. Take a fork and press the dough against the sides to seal it completely. Use a small, sharp knife to cut several $1\frac{1}{2}$-inch decorative slashes on the top of each crust. This will allow steam to escape.

To glaze and bake the pies: In a small bowl, combine the milk or cream with the egg yolk. Brush the tops of the pies with this mixture and bake for 15 minutes before turning the oven temperature down to 375°F and baking for another 30 minutes. If during the baking time the crusts appear to be browning too quickly, cover them loosely with foil.

Serve hot.

Cranberry Orange Turkey Breast

Serves 2 to 3 per pound

This practically no-fuss recipe will appeal to adults and children alike. It's a great alternative to whole roast turkey if you are serving friends and family who favor white meat. Making it ahead and refrigerating it overnight allows the flavors to meld and the juices to thicken slightly. Slicing is easier as well when the turkey is cold. Reheat in the microwave or in a roasting pan loosely covered with foil.

Leftovers make fabulous sandwiches.

1	fresh or defrosted uncooked whole turkey breast, with the skin on (if the kind you get has webbing on it, leave it on while the turkey cooks)
	Salt and freshly ground black pepper
4	large onions, peeled, cut in half, and cut into ½-inch slices
4	large carrots, peeled and cut into ¼-inch slices
4	cloves garlic, peeled and minced
2	cups dried apricots
2	cups dried cranberries
6	ounces orange juice concentrate, partially defrosted
1	10- to 12-ounce jar orange marmalade
2	cups canned chicken stock

Preheat the oven to 375°F, with the rack in the lower third of the oven but not the lowest position. Rinse the turkey breast and use paper towels to pat the skin dry. Place the breast, right-side up, in a heavy, shallow roasting pan and sprinkle with salt and pepper. Place the vegetables, apricots, and cranberries around the turkey.

Combine the orange juice concentrate, marmalade, and stock, mixing well. Pour the mixture over the vegetables and fruit in the pan. Roast, uncovered, for about 2 hours, or until the internal temperature registers 170°F. Cover the top loosely with foil if it seems to be browning too much.

Cut the turkey into thin slices to serve, garnishing it with cooked fruit and vegetables and spooning the sauce over all.

Grilled Brined Duck Breasts with Blackened Onion Relish

Serves 6

The Mayo Duck Farm in East Orleans is long gone, but just the mention of it will bring a smile to the face of many old-timers. My husband remembers not only the ducks sold for cooking but also the pet duckling that his parents (ill-advisedly) bought for his little sister. "It didn't end well," was all he was willing to say. It wasn't just ducks for sale, but desserts as well. "See if you can find that recipe for their Melt-a-Ways," begged one friend, who remembered a tender chocolate and mint cookie, the recipe for which seems to have disappeared with the place. This recipe is a tribute to a Cape Cod institution that lives in the hearts and stomachs of locals and tourists alike.

Duck cooked rare took a while to catch on in the States. While the French were enjoying this wonderfully tender, flavorful preparation, which tastes almost like aged steak, Americans were turning up their noses. Then came sushi, and rare duck didn't seem so strange after all.

After too many hours spent scrubbing duck fat from my oven and grease-slicked countertops, and one or two oven fires, I passionately believe that the very best place to cook duck is outside on the grill.

Using only the breast assures you of being able to cook the meat uniformly, so the skin is nice and crispy while the inside stays rosy. Soaking the duck in a brine (for at least 24 or as long as 48 hours) is well worth the time, as it brings out a whole new world of flavor.

For the duck

- 1½ cups water
- 1½ cups apple cider
- ½ cup coarse salt
- ½ cup (packed) dark brown sugar
- 2 tablespoons molasses
- 1 tablespoon peppercorns
- 1 tablespoon juniper berries
- 1 cinnamon stick
- 1 teaspoon whole cloves
  - Zest of 1 large lemon, coarsely grated
  - Juice of 1 lemon
- 6 duck breast halves (3 whole breasts, cut in half)

For the blackened onion relish

- 2 cloves garlic, peeled and minced
- ¼ cup soy sauce
- ½ cup vegetable oil
- ¼ cup balsamic vinegar
- 1 tablespoon prepared mustard
- 3 Vidalia or other sweet onions, peeled and cut into 1-inch rings

To brine the duck: Combine the water, cider, salt, brown sugar, molasses, peppercorns, juniper berries, cinnamon stick, cloves, and lemon zest and juice in a large saucepan set over high heat. Stir briefly while the mixture comes to a boil. Cook for 5 minutes, then remove from the heat and cool to room temperature.

Place the duck breasts in a shallow pan, and use a small, sharp knife to pierce the skin about 1/4 inch deep at 1-inch intervals. Add the brine (the cider/salt mixture) and turn the duck to coat both sides. Cover the pan with plastic wrap so that the plastic rests on the surface of the contents, and refrigerate for at least 24 hours and up to 48 hours, turning the pieces once or twice.

To grill the duck: I like to use a charcoal grill for this, but a gas grill is fine as long as the fire is very hot. If you do use charcoal, allow the coals to get white-hot before you begin to cook the duck. Remove the duck from the brine and use paper towels to wipe off any spices that might have adhered. Strain the brine mixture and reserve the liquid.

Grill the duck, skin-side down, for 20 minutes for medium-rare, turning the breasts every 4 to 5 minutes and basting with the strained liquid with every turn. Do not overcook! Remove the duck from the grill and allow it to rest for 10 minutes before slicing it on the diagonal across the grain.

To make the relish: Whisk the garlic, soy sauce, oil, vinegar, and mustard together in a shallow bowl. Add the onion rings and toss to coat. Allow the onions to sit at room temperature for at least 1 hour, or cover and refrigerate for up to 24 hours.

If you have room on the grill when the duck is cooking, remove the onion rings from the marinade, reserving the liquid. Place the onion rings around the duck and grill for 15 to 20 minutes, turning every 5 minutes and basting once or twice with the marinade, until the edges of the onions are black. How black you get them is a matter of taste—I like them really charred. Chop the cooked onions in large dice, and add a few tablespoons of the marinade just to moisten them.

To serve, fan the slices of duck out on dinner plates and arrange some of the onion relish on the side.

Millie's Oven-Fried Chicken

Serves 6

My mother makes the world's best oven-fried chicken. The recipe is so simple and easy that it's almost embarrassing—until you taste it. For picnics, she wraps each cooked and cooled piece in foil and sticks them in a cooler until the kids (blue-lipped and goosebumped from hours in the surf) come shivering up the sand to get wrapped in towels by clucking adults who just can't wait to stuff them full of lunch.

It makes sense, if you are feeding kids (and adults) straight from any beach activity, to make extra—it will disappear in seconds, and thirds.

You can buy cornflake crumbs, or you can make your own by placing cornflakes in a reclosable plastic bag and crushing them lightly with a rolling pin. Make sure the cornflakes aren't soggy or stale—and Millie suggests using Kellogg's.

4 pounds chicken parts (wings, breasts with bone in, drumsticks, thighs; see box)

1 16-ounce bottle prepared Italian dressing of your choice (Millie prefers Kraft)

3 cups cornflake crumbs

Salt and freshly ground black pepper

Rinse the chicken under cold running water and pat dry. Place the pieces in a large bowl, add the dressing, and toss to coat all the pieces. Cover with foil or plastic wrap and refrigerate for 24 hours.

Preheat the oven to 350°F, with the rack in the center position. Line a roasting pan with foil (for easy cleanup), or use a disposable foil roasting pan. Drain the chicken and discard the marinade. Place half the cornflake crumbs in a large plastic bag. Add the chicken pieces, 3 or 4 at a time, and toss to coat, patting the chicken through the bag to help the crumbs adhere.

Lay the chicken in the roasting pan (it's fine if the pieces touch), and repeat the breading process with the other pieces, adding additional crumbs as needed. Sprinkle any remaining crumbs on top of the chicken in the pan. Season with salt and pepper to taste. Bake for about 40 minutes (this will depend on the size of the chicken pieces), or until the juices run clear when the tip of a knife is inserted in the meat and the tops are crisp and browned.

Wrap the chicken in foil (1 or 2 pieces in a package), and refrigerate until ready to serve (or pack).

I find that thighs and drumsticks stay much more tender and moist than chicken breasts when baked this way—and they're more flavorful as well.

Grilled Bluefish with Mustard and Lime

Serves 6

The assertive taste and substantial texture of bluefish allows it to stand up to the flavor of the Dijon mustard in this quick, easy recipe. The fish can be prepared up to 6 hours ahead, covered, and refrigerated until ready to cook.

3   pounds bluefish fillets, skin removed

½   cup Dijon mustard

     Juice of 2 limes

2   cups fresh breadcrumbs

2   tablespoons chopped fresh rosemary leaves, or
     2 teaspoons dried rosemary

2   teaspoons sea salt

½   teaspoon freshly ground black pepper

Run your fingers over the surface of the bluefish to locate any remaining bones. Use a pair of tweezers to remove them. Cut the fillets into 6 pieces and place them in one layer in a large, shallow, disposable foil pan. In a small bowl, stir together the mustard and lime juice. Spread this mixture over the surface of the fish. Mix together the breadcrumbs, rosemary, salt, and pepper and sprinkle over the fish. Cover and refrigerate while you heat the grill.

When the coals are hot, place the foil pan on the grill. Cover and cook for 30 to 40 minutes, or until the fish flakes easily when tested with a sharp knife. Arrange the fish on a serving plate or individual dinner plates and serve immediately. The fish is also great served cold the next day.

You can bake the fish in the oven as well. Bake it in a pre-heated 375°F oven for 30 to 40 minutes, until cooked through.

Bacalhau *(Portuguese Salt Cod)*

Serves 8

Family names of Costa, Silva, Cook, and Souza are as familiar on the outer Cape as the Portuguese dishes that were carried to this country by seamen who followed the cod from the Azores to New England's coast.

I found dozens of recipes for this traditional dish. Each person of Portuguese descent that I asked had very strong opinions as well. There are recipes that call for adding olives to the mix, which I found makes it too salty. Instead, I added extra cream and a little cheese. The result is a little bit of the best of all of them. I imagine that purists will find my version a bit subtler than what they are used to, since I used less of the strong-tasting salt cod than is typical.

Salt cod is available in the fish section of many supermarkets, in fish stores, and in ethnic food stores. It must be soaked before using, not only to tenderize it but also to remove some of the briny taste.

This dish is extremely rich and filling. I usually serve it at breakfast with eggs, or as a starter before a light dinner.

1 pound salt cod

4 to 5 cups milk

6 tablespoons unsalted butter

2 large Spanish onions, peeled and minced

2 stalks celery, thinly sliced

3 large cloves garlic, peeled and minced

1½ cups Quick Fish Stock (page 206) or clam juice

½ cup dry white wine

2 cups heavy cream

3 pounds potatoes, peeled and cut into ¼-inch slices, simmered until just tender and drained

½ cup unseasoned breadcrumbs

½ cup grated Parmesan or Swiss cheese

Finely chopped flat-leaf (Italian) parsley leaves for garnish

Place the salt cod in a bowl, add water to cover, and refrigerate for 24 hours, changing the water 3 or 4 times, until the fish is soft. Discard the water and pat the fish dry. Place the cod in a large saucepan; cut it if necessary to fit. Cover with milk and bring to a simmer. Continue to simmer, uncovered, for 45 minutes to 1 hour, until the fish is very soft, adding additional milk as necessary to keep the fish submerged. When the fish is soft, drain it and discard the milk. When the fish is cool enough to handle, pat it dry, then use a fork to separate it into large (1½-inch) pieces. Remove and discard any skin and bones.

Butter the sides and bottom of a 3-quart ovenproof baking dish. Set aside.

Melt 3 tablespoons of the butter in a large, deep sauté pan over medium heat. Cook the onions and celery, stirring occasionally, for about 15 minutes, or until soft. Add the garlic and cook for another 3 to 4 minutes, stirring constantly so that the garlic doesn't brown. Pour in the fish stock or clam juice and wine and boil over high heat until the mixture is reduced by half. Add the cream and continue to boil for about 20 minutes, or until the mixture has reduced to 4 cups.

Preheat the oven to 325°F, with the rack in the center position. Spoon ¼ cup of the reduced cream mixture into the bottom of the prepared baking dish. Place half the potatoes in the dish so that they overlap slightly, ladle about 1 cup of the cream mixture over the potatoes, then cover evenly with the fish. Layer the remaining potatoes over the fish, then pour the rest of the cream mixture over all.

Place the breadcrumbs in a small bowl. Melt the remaining 3 tablespoons butter and pour it over the crumbs. Add the grated cheese and stir to mix well. Scatter the crumb mixture over the contents of the baking dish. Bake, uncovered, for 50 to 60 minutes, or until the cream bubbles, a knife inserted in the center comes out hot, and the top is crusty and brown. Serve hot, garnished with a sprinkling of chopped parsley.

Bacalhau with Fried Eggs

Serves 2

Here's the answer to the question "What do I do with that little bit of leftover bacalhau?"

2   cups hot Bacalhau (facing page)

4   extra-large eggs, fried over-easy

    Salsa (purchased or homemade) for topping

Spoon a cup of hot bacalhau onto the center of each of 2 warm plates. Slide 2 eggs on top of each serving, and top with a tablespoon or two of salsa.

Cod Baked with Oven-Roasted Tomatoes

Serves 6

The great thing about this fish preparation, besides the zesty flavor and colorful presentation, is that components of it, such as the oven-roasted tomatoes and the onion and bell peppers, can be prepared well ahead of time so that the final preparation takes just a few minutes. Another great feature is that, like most baked fish dishes, it can be prepared either in the oven or in a baking dish on the grill.

¼	cup olive oil
1	large Vidalia onion, peeled, cut in half, and thinly sliced
3	cloves garlic, peeled and minced
1	large yellow bell pepper, cut in half, seeded, cored, and cut into ¼-inch dice
1	large orange bell pepper, cut in half, seeded, cored, and cut into ¼-inch dice
2	cups Oven-Roasted Tomatoes (page 203)
⅓	cup pitted green olives, coarsely chopped
	Salt and freshly ground black pepper
3	pounds cod fillets, cut from the thick end

Heat the oil in a large skillet set over medium-high heat. Sauté the onion until limp, about 10 minutes, stirring occasionally. Lower the heat to medium, add the garlic, and cook for 5 minutes, stirring frequently to prevent the garlic from browning. Add the bell peppers and cook for 20 minutes, or until they are soft but not mushy. Remove the pan from the heat and stir in the tomatoes and olives. Add salt and pepper to taste.

Preheat the oven to 375°F, or light the grill. If you are using the oven, lightly coat a shallow, ovenproof baking dish large enough to hold the fish in one layer with vegetable oil. If you are using the grill, arrange the fish in the same manner in a disposable foil pan. Spoon the sauce over the fish and bake it in the oven or in a covered grill for about 30 minutes, or until the fish flakes easily when tested in the center of the fillet with a fork or small, sharp knife.

Broiled Gravlax

Serves 8

In this dish, you "cure" the salmon by rubbing it with a mixture of salt, white pepper, and sugar, then packing it in dill and placing it under weights for several days. In Scandinavia (and in this country as well), the fish is then eaten as is (cured, but uncooked). Here, however, the cured fish is broiled on just one side, leaving the top crusty and brown and the interior rare. It's one of my most favorite fish preparations, because not only does it taste and look sensational but all the work is done well ahead and the actual cooking takes no time at all, leaving you free to be a guest at your own party.

For curing the salmon

2	4-pound salmon fillets, skin removed
¼	cup brandy or aquavit
⅓	cup coarse sea or kosher salt
⅓	cup granulated sugar
1	teaspoon freshly ground white pepper
3	large bunches fresh dill, well rinsed and dried, the roots but not the stems removed

For broiling the salmon

⅔	cup (packed) dark brown sugar
⅓	cup Dijon mustard
2	tablespoons soy sauce
	Juice and finely grated zest of 2 limes
	Dill sprigs for garnish

To cure the salmon: Run your fingers over the fish and locate any remaining bones. Use tweezers to pull them out. Pat the fish dry, then rub both sides with the brandy or aquavit.

Mix the salt, sugar, and pepper together in a small bowl. Select a large, rimmed baking sheet or shallow roasting pan large enough to accommodate the length one of the fillets, with a little room to spare. Lay 2 sheets of heavy-duty aluminum foil that measure 4 inches longer than the fish on the counter so that they are slightly overlapping lengthwise. Take 1 bunch of dill and lay it on the foil, covering an area the size of one of the fillets.

continued

120

Gently rub 1 tablespoon of the salt mixture into each side of both fillets. Discard any remaining salt mixture. Lay one of the fillets, skinned-side down, on the dill bed. Take a second bunch of dill and arrange it on top of the fillet. Cover this with the second fillet (skinned-side up), and then finally add the last bunch of dill. Gather the sides and ends of the foil and encase the fish tightly and completely. Wrap the bundle in several more sheets of foil, pressing the package tightly closed.

Place the wrapped fish in the pan and place a baking sheet or tray on top. On the upper tray, place some heavy cans or an iron or other weight. I actually use a marble rolling pin, along with some large cans of stewed tomatoes. See if you can get at least 5 to 7 pounds on top of the fish. Refrigerate for at least 3 days, and no longer than 5 days, in the coldest part of the refrigerator, turning the fish every day and draining off any accumulated liquid from the pan.

To broil the salmon: Mix together the sugar, mustard, soy sauce, lime juice, and zest in a small bowl and set aside. Preheat the broiler, with the rack in the upper third of the oven but not the highest position. Remove the fish from the foil. Remove and discard the dill. Use a sharp knife to cut each fillet into 4 pieces, and place them close together but not touching on a foil-lined heavy-duty rimmed baking sheet. Coat the top of each piece of fish generously with the brown sugar mixture. Broil for 5 to 6 minutes on one side only, until the surface of the fish is bubbling and crisp and the fish is cooked about halfway through but is still very rare inside. While you can certainly continue cooking the fish until it is completely cooked through, you will lose the sublime taste and texture that comes from the curing.

Serve hot, garnished with a sprig of fresh dill.

Sea Bass Poached in Ginger Fish Broth with Cilantro Pesto

Serves 6

Sea bass is tender and flavorful and, most important, sturdy enough to be steamed without falling apart. In this recipe, created for my son Max, fragrant ginger-infused shrimp broth surrounds the lovely white fish, along with accents of yellow and green from both kinds of squash, the bright red of the cherry tomatoes, and the vivid green of the cilantro pesto. The broth can be made a day ahead and kept refrigerated until ready to use. The same is true for the cilantro pesto.

For the shrimp broth

- 3 tablespoons olive oil
- 2 yellow onions, peeled and cut into 1/2-inch dice
- 3 carrots, peeled and chopped
- 3 stalks celery with leaves, cut into 1/2-inch dice
- 3 cloves garlic, peeled and coarsely chopped
- 3 tablespoons fresh ginger, peeled and coarsely chopped
- 8 ounces shrimp, in the shell
- 4 anchovies in oil
- 2 cups dry white wine
- 10 cups water
- 1 cup clam juice (fresh, bottled, or reconstituted)
- 1/4 cup lemon juice

   Salt and freshly ground black pepper

For the pesto

- 1 cup cilantro leaves
- 2 cloves garlic, peeled
- 1 tablespoon freshly grated lemon zest
- 1 teaspoon coarse salt
- 1/2 cup mild olive oil, plus 1 tablespoon for drizzling

For poaching the fish

- 1 cup clam juice (fresh, bottled, or reconstituted)
- 1 cup water
- 24 littleneck clams
- 3 pounds boneless sea bass, cut into six 8-ounce portions
- 4 small, tender zucchini, cut into small dice
- 4 small, tender yellow squash, cut into small dice
- 6 Red Bliss or new potatoes, cut into 1/2-inch slices and steamed until just tender
- 2 cups cherry tomatoes, halved

continued

To make the shrimp broth: Heat the oil in a large saucepan set over high heat. Add the onions, carrots, and celery and cook for 5 to 7 minutes, stirring frequently with a wooden or heatproof plastic spoon, until the onions are limp and just beginning to turn golden. Lower the heat to medium and add the garlic. Cook for 2 more minutes, stirring frequently to avoid letting the garlic turn brown. Add the ginger, shrimp, and anchovies and cook for 5 minutes, continuing to stir occasionally. Add the white wine and stir the mixture, scraping the bottom of the pot. Bring the mixture to a simmer and cook until the wine is reduced by two-thirds. Add the water and clam juice, bring to a boil, and turn the heat down to a simmer. Simmer, uncovered, for 45 minutes over low heat. Add the lemon juice and continue to simmer until you have about 8 cups of liquid. Season with salt and pepper to taste. Strain the broth through cheesecloth or a fine-mesh sieve. You should have 8 cups. If you are not proceeding with the rest of the recipe until later, pour the broth into a metal bowl, cover with foil, and refrigerate immediately. Since the shrimp have given up all their flavor to the stock, they will now be tasteless (and tough) and should be discarded.

To make the pesto: Add the cilantro, garlic, lemon zest, and salt to the work bowl of a food processor fitted with the metal blade. Pulse to combine. With the motor running, pour the olive oil through the feed tube in a slow, steady stream, processing until it is absorbed. Pour and scrape the mixture into a small plastic container. Drizzle a tablespoon of olive oil onto the surface and place a piece of plastic wrap over and touching the surface, to keep the mixture from discoloring.

To poach the fish: Add the clam juice and water to a large pot placed over high heat. When the mixture comes to a rapid boil, add the clams, cover, and return to a gentle simmer. Cook for 10 to 12 minutes, or until the clams open. Remove the pan from the heat and keep it covered while you prepare the fish.

Bring the shrimp broth to a gentle simmer in a large skillet. Add the fish, cover the pan, and cook at a gentle simmer until the fish is cooked through, 15 to 18 minutes. Add the zucchini, yellow squash, potatoes, and cherry tomatoes at the very end of the cooking time and simmer for 1 or 2 minutes, until the vegetables are al dente.

Use a slotted spoon to place a piece of fish and some of the vegetables in each of 6 rimmed soup plates or shallow bowls. Place 4 clams around the edge of the fish and spoon the hot broth over all. Top with a dollop of cilantro pesto.

Slow-Cooked Striped Bass

Serves 6

The striped bass season is short, both to protect the supply and to give fishermen time to think about something else while they wait for the day when they can get up before dawn and stand with dozens of their compatriots, surf-casting for treasure. July finds all sorts of folks, clutching long poles, on the beach and in boats, watching the sunrise while they try for a big one. Chances are very good that if you didn't get that striper from your next-door neighbor, you got it from the fish store, which got it from your next-door neighbor.

This leisurely preparation perfumes the house with the fragrant aroma of fresh herbs and lemon. The result is the most succulent and flavorful fish dish I've ever had—it's one of my favorite ways of preparing my favorite fish. Don't be alarmed at the amount of olive oil—it's not a mistake.

While this fish is heavenly right out of the oven, you should also consider serving it cold with a side of salad greens. Use some of the olive oil from the cooking to make a vinaigrette or homemade mayonnaise. It makes a perfect lunch or light supper.

2½ to 3 cups olive oil

2 shallots, peeled and minced

1 large bunch fresh thyme (about 20 sprigs)

6 sprigs fresh rosemary

3 lemons, thinly sliced and seeded

3 limes, thinly sliced

3 pounds striped bass fillets, skin removed

2 teaspoons sea salt

Freshly ground black pepper

Preheat the oven to 275°F, with the rack in the center position. Select an ovenproof baking dish, casserole, or roasting pan large enough to hold the fish in one layer comfortably. Pour half of the olive oil on the bottom of the pan and spread to cover. Sprinkle the shallots over the oil, then arrange half of the thyme sprigs and half of the rosemary over the shallots. Cover these with half of the lemon and lime slices, overlapping if necessary to cover an area the size of the fillets. Lay the fillets over the lemons and limes, and cover them first with the remaining herbs, then with the remaining lemon and limes slices. Drizzle the remaining olive oil over all, adding more if necessary to submerge all but the top surface of the fillets. Sprinkle with the sea salt and pepper to taste, and cover loosely with foil. Bake for 1 hour, then remove the foil and bake for an additional 30 minutes, or until the fish flakes very easily when tested with a fork.

Serve hot or cold.

Baked Stuffed Lobster

Serves 6

The Brody family celebrated Julia Child's move from Cambridge, Massachusetts, to Santa Barbara, California, with a New England dinner—just to remind her of what she'd be missing. Julia loved the Maine oysters (topped with osetra caviar), and the Cranberry-Pear Linzertorte (page 174), but the high point of the meal was the baked stuffed lobsters prepared by my son Max and his great friend Pete Hickock. These two were in the same graduation class at the Culinary Institute of America and were as overjoyed to cook dinner for Julia as she was to eat their creation.

This lobster is prepared for easy eating—all the work is done for you. Don't turn your nose up at the Ritz cracker stuffing—it's genuine, classic, and rates a perfect score on the taste-o-meter.

You can find fresh (cooked) Maine crabmeat in a fish store or the seafood department of your grocery store. Some stores also carry imported crabmeat from Thailand, which is an acceptable substitute. Don't make the mistake of buying crab legs or surimi.

The lobsters can be stuffed up to 8 hours ahead and refrigerated, lightly covered in plastic wrap, until ready to cook. If you do this, add 10 minutes to the baking time to make sure they are heated all the way through.

6   live lobsters, 1½ pounds each

1   cup (2 sticks) unsalted butter, melted and slightly cooled

3   cups crushed Ritz Crackers

2   pounds fresh crabmeat, picked over to remove any cartilage

3   tablespoons dry sherry

3   tablespoons lemon juice

¼   cup chopped fresh parsley

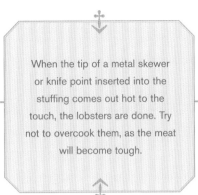

When the tip of a metal skewer or knife point inserted into the stuffing comes out hot to the touch, the lobsters are done. Try not to overcook them, as the meat will become tough.

Bring a large pot of salted water to a rapid boil. Add the lobsters, 3 at a time, cover the pot, and bring the water back to the boil. Simmer for 8 minutes, then immediately rinse the lobsters with cold water to stop the cooking. Repeat with the other 3 lobsters.

Place a lobster on its back on a towel. First remove the claws and knuckles from the body and reserve. With kitchen shears or scissors, carefully cut open the tail on either side of the underbelly to remove the cartilage covering the tail meat. Firmly holding the lobster body, remove the legs and the upper body by pulling up on the inner carcass, being careful not to separate the body shell from the tail shell. Remove the legs and reserve them for garnish. Remove the tail meat from the shell in one piece. Rinse the green tomalley from the tail meat (reserving it for another purpose or discarding it), and gently clean the shell with a damp paper towel. Remove the meat from the claws, and remove the knuckle shell and the cartilage from the claws. Coarsely chop the lobster meat and reserve.

In a large mixing bowl, add the melted butter to the crushed Ritz crackers. Add the crabmeat, sherry, and lobster meat and fold together with a rubber spatula until well incorporated.

Preheat the oven to 350°F, with the rack in the center position. Select a roasting pan large enough to hold all the lobster bodies. Spoon the stuffing mixture into the lobster shell, and place the lobsters in the pan. Bake for 20 minutes, or until heated through and browned on top (see box). Place a lobster on each serving plate and drizzle with lemon juice and sprinkle with parsley. Garnish with the reserved legs.

Boiled Lobster

Serves 4

I've eaten lobster cooked every imaginable way, and when it comes right down to it, there is nothing to equal the K.I.S.S. formula (keep it simple, sweetheart). Boiling works because it's easy to figure out from a timing formula when the lobster is done. And doneness is one of the keys to great lobster. Undercooked lobster is unappetizing (at best), and overcooked lobster is tough and stringy.

Here are some other keys to attaining lobster greatness:

Freshness: I try to buy the lobsters the day I plan to cook them, transporting them home in a cooler (not a paper sack thrown in the trunk of the car). Look for firm- to hard-shelled, vigorously active lobsters that move energetically when lifted from the tank.

Storage: When you get the lobsters home, keep them either in the cooler, packed with the kind of freezer packs that are not likely to puncture if clipped by a lobster's claw, in a loosely closed insulated paper bag that comes from the fish market, or wrapped in newspaper. Don't store them in plastic bags or wrap them in plastic. Cook them within 24 hours.

Source: Don't be shy about asking where the lobsters come from. Obviously, East Coast lobsters are going to be the best, and lobsters from a fish market are probably going to be fresher and of a higher quality than those at a chain supermarket.

Size: When gauging the size of the lobsters to buy, take into account your family's and guests' appetites and what else you plan to serve. Lobster is rich and filling, and while it's nice to have plenty, throwing any away would be a shame (unless, of course, you rescue it for lobster salad or lobster rolls the next day). It would also be a shame not to have room for corn on the cob and dessert.

Restaurateur and lobster maven Jasper White, in his wonderful book *Lobster at Home,* suggests cooking lobster in seawater. He says, "It is the briny-sweet taste of the sea, where all life began, that is so intensely satisfying and sensually stimulating." Who am I to argue with someone who knows more about cooking fish than anyone I know? If you don't have access to seawater, you'll have to settle for salted water (1/4 cup salt per gallon of water).

You want to cook the lobsters in plenty of water, so select a very large stockpot that will hold the water with enough head room to accommodate the lobsters. Or use two smaller pots, or cook the lobsters two at a time.

Don't forget to set the table with tools of the trade, including heavy-duty nut (or claw) crackers, long thin picks for extracting meat from hard-to-access places, a large bowl for shells, and plenty of napkins or paper towels. By the way, lobster bibs are for tourists.

3   gallons seawater, or 3 gallons tap water plus ¾ cup sea salt

4   live lobsters, 1¼ to 2 pounds each

     Lobster Butter (page 201) or melted unsalted butter for serving

     Lemon wedges for serving

In a large, covered pot set over high heat, bring the water to a rolling boil. Add the lobsters, cover, and cook for 10 minutes for 1¼-pound lobsters, 12 minutes for 1½-pound lobsters, and 15 minutes for 2-pound lobsters. Start timing the cooking when the lobsters go into the pot.

Use tongs to remove the lobsters from the pot, draining them by holding them over the pot for a moment before placing them on either a platter or individual plates. Use a small, sharp knife to slit open the tail.

Serve with Lobster Butter or melted butter and lemon wedges.

There are people who insist on serving clarified butter with their lobster. This is butter from which the milky white residue (milk solids) has been removed. I agree with Jasper White, who says that it's this oft-discarded component that gives butter its flavor and that it should be left right where it is. If you do want to make clarified butter, there are several ways to do so. You can melt the butter in a microwave (be sure to cover the container tightly, as those same milk solids tend to explode all over the microwave when they boil) and pour off the golden butter, leaving the milk solids behind. Or you can put the butter in a pan set over high heat and bring it to a boil. The milk solids will rise to the top and begin to evaporate. Skim them off with a small spoon until they are completely gone. Be sure to cool the butter down to tepid before serving it along with the lobster.

Lobster Rolls

Makes 2

There is something almost magical about the combination of a buttery, toasted hot dog bun, the crunch of a tender lettuce leaf, and the sublime richness of chunks of fresh lobster. Some folks have tried to fancy up this Cape Cod classic with herbed dressing or spice-infused homemade mayonnaise, but I say give me Hellman's any day.

I find that the salt content in the mayonnaise is plenty for me, but if you like more, then feel free to add it. Pepperidge Farm hot dog rolls are my favorite because they have more substance than the generic grocery-store brands.

1   pound freshly cooked lobster meat, tail and claw, cut into 1-inch pieces

⅓   cup prepared mayonnaise

    Juice of 1 small lemon

    Freshly ground black pepper

2   tablespoons butter

2   split-top hot dog rolls

2   to 4 leaves Boston lettuce, rinsed and patted dry

Place the lobster in a medium-sized mixing bowl. Stir in the mayonnaise and lemon juice and season with pepper to taste.

Melt the butter in a skillet set over high heat, and when it is sizzling, add the hot dog rolls, coating each side with butter. Cook the rolls on each side, pressing them lightly with a flat spatula, until they are crisp and brown. You also have the option of splitting the rolls open at this point and browning the exposed area.

Line the rolls with the lettuce, pile in the lobster, and serve immediately with chips and a dill pickle spear.

Beer-Fried Oysters

Serves 6 as an appetizer, 4 as a main course

Next to eating them raw with a squeeze of lemon, this is my favorite way to enjoy oysters. Sometimes if oysters are large, they are better fried than served raw (I think raw oysters should be small enough to be eaten in one bite). These need to be consumed immediately after they are made, so be sure to make the tartar sauce first.

2   dozen oysters, shucked (see pages 54–55), the larger, the better

1   cup oyster cracker crumbs

¼   cup beer

1   extra-large egg, slightly beaten

½   teaspoon salt

Freshly ground black pepper

1   cup solid vegetable shortening

Tartar Sauce (page 197) for serving

Lemon wedges for serving

Drain the oysters of their liquid, and then dry them well with paper towels. Line a tray with paper towels. Place the cracker crumbs in a shallow bowl. Mix the beer, egg, salt, and pepper to taste in a second bowl. Melt the shortening in a medium-width but deep skillet or electric frying pan. The shortening should be 1½ to 2 inches deep, or deep enough so that the oysters are completely submerged. Dip the oysters one at a time into the egg mixture and then into the crumbs, rolling them around to coat them completely. Use a slotted spoon to lower them into the hot fat, cooking only 3 or 4 at a time. Cook for 1 to 1½ minutes, until golden brown. Use the slotted spoon to transfer the cooked oysters to the paper towel–lined tray to drain. Serve immediately with tartar sauce and lemon wedges.

Clambakes

Outdoor Clambake

Serves 8

There are companies that dedicate themselves to putting on clambakes for other people (paying customers). Companies like this stay in business because, while the idea of a clambake on the beach is a great one, the execution is a pretty daunting endeavor. Lest you be deprived of the opportunity to stage your own clambake, instructions for the outdoor version follow. If you are like me and eagerly await an invitation to someone else's clambake (at which they do all the work), you might want to check out the directions for the much simpler indoor version that follows.

By the way, if you are visiting the Cape for the first time or are new to bonfires, make sure to secure a permit from the town before you strike any matches.

You'll need *large* amounts of the following (this is where having energetic children who are willing to be bribed with ice cream come in handy).

Equipment

Shovels

Large rocks

Charcoal

Newspaper and kindling

Driftwood, firewood (nontreated, not pine)

Fresh seaweed

Large canvas tarp

Fireproof gloves

Food for the pit

8   live lobsters, 1½ to 2 pounds each

8   dozen cleaned steamers (see box, page 52)

8   ears corn on the cob, unshucked

2   pounds large shrimp, unshelled (optional)

3   pounds linguiça sausage (optional)

continued

Accompaniments and other essentials

Permit to build a fire on the beach

Cold beer

Chips

Garlic bread

Mosquito/no-see-um repellent if you are doing this
after sundown

Nutcrackers

Lobster picks

Melted butter for serving

Lemon wedges for serving

More beer

Take a look at all the stuff you have to cook (including the fuel for the fire), and dig a large pit in the sand to accommodate it. Line the pit with rocks. Place the charcoal on top of the rocks. Set the driftwood and firewood on top (tucking in the crumpled-up newspaper and kindling). Without using kerosene or fire starter (if possible), make a roaring *big* bonfire.

Start passing out the beer, chips, garlic bread, and insect repellent.

Allow the fire to burn (adding more wood and/or charcoal as necessary) for about 2 hours, or until the charcoal is red hot and the rocks are steaming. Cover the rocks with a thin layer of seaweed, and lay the lobsters in one layer over them. Add another layer of seaweed to cover the lobsters, then cover it with all the clams. More seaweed, then the corn, more seaweed, and then the shrimp, if desired. If using sausage, add it at this point as well. End with a 5-inch-thick layer of seaweed. Cover the entire pit with the canvas tarp and bake for 30 minutes, or until the corn is steamed through and the clams have opened.

Dig in and don't worry about getting yourself covered with food—that's why the ocean is there.

Lazy Man's Clambake

Serves 4

Now for a much more civilized approach to the concept of a clambake: one that is done indoors, over a stove in a room where there is a delightful mesh screen between you and the no-see-ums. If you don't have a lobster pot, you can use a very large Dutch oven or even the metal insert to a large chafing dish. Be creative—but just make sure that whatever you use is flameproof. I realize most people will find it hard to get seaweed, although fish-mongers sometimes have it to use in displays. You can substitute corn husks or lettuce leaves.

You will need the following:

Lots of damp seaweed, corn husks,
or lettuce leaves

4   cups beer

1   or 2 lobster pots (very large kettles)

4   live lobsters, 1½ pounds each

4   ears corn on the cob, husked, wrapped in foil

4   dozen steamers, cleaned (see box, page 52)

Melted butter for serving

Lemon wedges for serving

Sunset Slaw (page 96)

Place the seaweed, corn husks, or lettuce leaves in the bottom of the pot(s). Cover with the beer. Heat to a simmer (you might have to place the pot over 2 burners). Add the lobsters to the pot(s) and add enough seaweed, corn husks, or lettuce to just cover. Add the foil-wrapped corn and more seaweed, and finally add the clams. Cover with the remaining seaweed. Cover the pot(s) and cook over medium heat (you should be able to hear the liquid bubble gently) for 20 minutes, or until the clams open. Serve with melted butter, lemon wedges, and Sunset Slaw.

Grilled Sea Scallops *(Scallop Kabobs)*

Serves 6

When large sea scallops are available, this is the perfect recipe to use them in. It's important to remove the chewy muscle that holds the scallop to its shell. In this dish, those bits are used to enhance the sauce. You can make this either in the oven under the broiler or on the grill.

The sauce can be prepared up to the point at which the butter is added, up to 6 hours ahead of time, and refrigerated. You can finish the sauce after the scallops are cooked—it takes only a minute or two.

3   pounds sea scallops

For the marinade

¾   cup prepared mayonnaise

3   tablespoons dark brown sugar

1   tablespoon Dijon mustard

½   teaspoon mild Asian sesame oil

For the sauce

    Reserved scallop muscles

¾   cup white wine

½   cup water

⅓   cup balsamic vinegar

3   tablespoons soy sauce

1   large shallot, peeled and minced

2   stalks celery, cut into 1-inch pieces

3   tablespoons unsalted butter

To marinate the scallops: Rinse the scallops, pull off and reserve the muscles, and pat dry. In a small bowl, mix together the marinade ingredients. Add the scallops to a mixing bowl or large reclosable plastic bag, add the marinade, and stir to coat the scallops. Cover the bowl with plastic wrap or seal the plastic bag and refrigerate for at least 1 hour and as long as 6 hours.

To make the sauce: Combine everything but the butter in a medium-sized sauté pan set over moderate heat. Bring the mixture to a simmer and cook until the liquid is reduced by half. Use a slotted spoon to remove the scallop muscles, shallot, and celery. Just before serving, bring the sauce to a rapid simmer over high heat and whisk in the butter until the sauce has emulsified and is slightly thick.

To grill the scallops: Light a gas or charcoal grill, or preheat the broiler with the rack in the highest position. Soak 6 to 8 wooden skewers (the number you need will depend on the length of the skewers) in water for 15 to 20 minutes to prevent the scallops from sticking. Slide the scallops onto the skewers from one side through the other (not through the top and bottom), so that they touch one another with no space in between. Grill for 6 to 7 minutes on each side, or broil for 3 to 4 minutes on each side, or just until the edges are nicely browned and the scallops are no longer translucent inside. Try not to overcook the scallops, as it will make them tough. Use a fork to slide the scallops onto individual plates, and drizzle each serving with a tablespoon or two of the sauce.

Leslie Revsin's
Sautéed Cod with Capers

Serves 4

When my good friend, the talented restaurateur and cookbook author, Leslie Revsin, published her first book, *Great Fish Quick*, I knew the answer to "What's for dinner?" was solved, especially when I am looking for something slightly inventive to do with cod. Not only will this dish make it to the table in 30 minutes—start to finish—but I will guarantee rave reviews.

Leslie advises that this can also be made with sole, haddock, hake, pollack, cusk, orange roughy, halibut, bass, or snapper fillets.

1	extra-large egg, beaten with 2 tablespoons cold water
4	7-ounce cod fillets, each about 1 inch thick
	Salt and freshly ground black or white pepper
¾	cup flour for dredging
2	teaspoons vegetable oil
2	tablespoons butter
2	tablespoons white wine or dry vermouth
1	tablespoon drained capers

Preheat the oven to 350°F, with the rack in the upper third of the oven but not the highest position. Place the beaten egg in a shallow container large enough to dip 1 cod fillet. Season the fillets with salt and pepper. Place the flour on a plate or in a shallow baking dish.

Place a large, ovenproof skillet over low heat and add the vegetable oil. Meanwhile, dredge both sides of each fillet in the flour and pat off the excess. Place the floured fillets, one at a time, in the beaten egg, turning them to coat both sides. Set them aside on a plate as you finish each one.

Turn the heat under the skillet to medium-high and add the butter. When the butter is melted and frothing, slip the fillets into the skillet, round-side down. Sauté the fillets for 4 to 5 minutes, until they are golden brown on the bottom, lowering the heat if they are browning too quickly. Use a metal spatula to turn them over, and then place the skillet in the preheated oven.

Bake the fillets until cooked through, milky white and opaque throughout, and still moist—about 10 minutes. To check, slip one edge of your spatula into the thickest part of a fillet and gently separate part of it. It shouldn't offer any resistance. If necessary, return the skillet to the oven and bake for another few minutes.

Remove the cooked fillets to a heated platter (reserve the cooking liquid in the skillet), and keep them warm by covering them with foil while you make the sauce. Pour the white wine or vermouth into the skillet and set it over high heat. Boil the liquid, adding any juices that have collected on the platter and scraping up any brown bits that have stuck to the skillet. Cook until you have about 3 tablespoons. Turn off the heat, stir in the capers, and season with salt and pepper, if needed.

Place the cod on warm dinner plates, spoon some of the sauce on top of each, and serve immediately.

Mussels Three Ways

In our house we feel that the less done in the preparation of mussels the better. Hot, right from the shell is the way we like them. Any of the following three recipes will deliver up a tasty mussel dinner with a minimum of fuss and maximum flavor.

One step that cannot be avoided is cleaning and debearding the mussels. To do this, dump the mussels into a large colander or right into the sink. Rinse thoroughly with cold running water (or use a scrub brush if the mussels are particularly gritty or covered with barnacles). Discard any mussels that are cracked or opened. Use your fingers to grasp the tough threads that are at the hinge end of the shell, and pull them off and discard them. This takes a little practice, but you'll get the hang of it.

A good rule of thumb is to count on 1-plus quart of mussels in their shells per person for a dinner-sized portion. This will give you about a cup of meat. These recipes are written for six people but are easily adjustable up or downward. Don't be tempted, however, to pile them more than 8 to 10 inches deep in any cooking vessel, as the ones on the bottom will have trouble opening and will finish cooking before the ones on the top. To avoid this, you can make several batches—which shouldn't be a big deal since the cooking time is fast. I always like to make extra mussels, since they are great cold the next day.

Mussels Steamed with Wine and Garlic

Serves 6

If you've stayed at the beach or in the garden right up until dinnertime and are facing a hungry crowd, think mussels. Usually a fraction of the price of other shellfish, and quick and easy to prepare, they look beautiful on the plate with their deep black-blue shells and delicate pink meat. Eating them is a hands-on activity, so have plenty of napkins available.

2   cups dry white wine

2   large shallots, peeled and minced

4   large cloves garlic, peeled and minced

2   bay leaves

6   quarts mussels, cleaned and debearded as described above

1/3   cup finely chopped flat-leaf (Italian) parsley

1/2   cup (1 stick) butter, cut into several pieces

Combine the wine, shallots, garlic, and bay leaves in a very large skillet set over high heat. Bring the mixture to a rapid simmer and cook for 5 minutes. Add the mussels and cover the skillet. If you don't have a large enough cover, use a baking sheet. When the liquid returns to a boil, reduce the heat and simmer the mussels for 5 minutes, shaking the pot to distribute the contents. Cook for another minute or so, then remove the lid and use a slotted spoon to remove the mussels that have opened. Cover again and cook for another 2 to 3 minutes. Remove all the mussels, discarding those that have not opened. Strain the cooking liquid through a mesh sieve. Return the liquid to the skillet (rinsed to remove any sand or grit), and cook over high heat until about 1½ cups remain. Add the parsley and butter, whisking until the butter melts.

To serve, distribute the mussels among 6 shallow bowls, and add some of the cooking liquid to each bowl. Serve hot.

Bonfire Mussels

Serves 6

The next time you plan a bonfire on the beach and you want something either different from or to augment your traditional clambake fare, try this.

Try not to fill the pot more than 8 to 10 inches deep at a time. To avoid this, you may have to cook the mussels in batches. The cooking time is very short. No additional liquid is added to this recipe.

6   quarts mussels, cleaned and debearded as
    described on facing page

    Melted butter for serving

Add the mussels to a very large kettle (or 2 kettles). Cover and set over the fire. Shake the pan several times to distribute the mussels. Cook, covered, for 5 to 7 minutes, or until they have opened and are cooked through. Serve hot, passing the melted butter for dipping.

Grilled Mussels

Serves 6

A wire basket made to go on the grill will make this easy recipe even easier.

6   quarts mussels, cleaned and debearded as
    described on facing page

    Melted butter for serving

Light a gas or charcoal fire. Place the mussels in either a wire basket or a disposable aluminum pan. Don't pile them more than 8 to 10 inches high. Cover the grill and cook for 10 to 15 minutes, or until the mussels have opened. They probably won't all open at the same time, but make sure to discard any that don't open after 20 minutes of cooking.

Serve hot, passing the butter for dipping.

Steamed Clams

Serves 4 to 6

Every Cape Codder knows that the very best way to enjoy clams is straight from the pot after they have simply been steamed open. Dipped in clam broth and then in butter, they are an experience that makes you wish summer lasted all year long.

You can steam both hard- and soft-shell clams. The soft-shell clams (steamers) are the ones with the long neck, tender belly, and a propensity for grit that must be purged before they are cooked. Hard-shell clams (littlenecks and cherrystones) are chewier and don't have necks. It's a personal thing, so try them both and make up your own mind which you prefer.

This recipe can also be used to steam mussels.

1   cup white wine

1   cup clam juice

1   medium onion, peeled and sliced

2   stalks celery with leaves, cut into 1-inch slices

6   dozen hard-shell clams, rinsed; soft-shell clams, cleaned and purged (page 52); or mussels, rinsed and debearded (page 140)

½   cup (1 stick) butter, melted

Place the liquids, onion, and celery in a large pot set over high heat. When the liquid comes to a rapid boil, add the shellfish, cover the pot, and reduce the heat to a gentle simmer. Cook for 6 to 9 minutes, or until the shells have opened. Pour the cooking liquid through a fine-mesh strainer (or several layers of cheesecloth) into a serving bowl. Discard any shellfish that have not opened, and serve the remaining ones hot along with the broth and a bowl of melted butter in which to dip them.

Spaghetti Foriana Ciro and Sal's

Serves 4

Down at the end of Kiley Court in Provincetown's East End, there's an institution well loved by generations of residents and visitors alike. Although Ciro no longer owns it and Sal has long since departed for his own place in the West End, and there are not quite so many straw-covered Chianti bottles and metal graters hanging from the ceiling, you can still on rare occasion see Norman Mailer eating in a dark corner, and you can still order Spaghetti Foriana.

It says on the menu that this dish comes from the island of Ischia, which is near Capri in the Tyrrhenian Sea. I've been to Ischia, and I never ate anything there as wonderful as this pasta. The combination of raisins, nuts, and anchovies may strike you as strange, but trust me: The combination of salt and sweet is magnificent.

The sauce needs to be made just before serving, so have all the ingredients ready and make it while the spaghetti is cooking.

¾ cup olive oil

4 cloves garlic, peeled and minced

9 anchovy fillets, drained (oil reserved) and patted dry, divided

½ cup pine nuts, lightly toasted

½ cup walnuts, broken into large pieces

½ cup raisins

1 teaspoon dried oregano

Pinch hot red pepper flakes

¼ teaspoon freshly ground black pepper

1½ pounds spaghetti, cooked al dente

⅓ cup chopped fresh flat-leaf (Italian) parsley, leaves only

Freshly grated Parmesan cheese

In a large sauté pan set over medium heat, heat the oil. Add the garlic and cook for 2 to 3 minutes, stirring frequently to prevent burning. Add 9 of the anchovy fillets, mashing with a wooden spoon until they dissolve. Add the nuts, raisins, oregano, pepper flakes, and black pepper and cook for 4 minutes more, shaking the pan and/or stirring to move the contents around. Add the cooked pasta and the parsley. Toss to combine, garnish with remaining 4 anchovy fillets, and serve immediately. Pass the cheese on the side.

Spaghetti with White Clam Sauce

Serves 4

While some people like to make this with clams still in the shell, I think folks should be able to get down to the business of eating the pasta—not wasting time fishing clams out of hot shells while their pasta gets cold. Thus, I start with chopped clams, which are available at most fish markets and many supermarkets.

For the sauce

- ½ cup (1 stick) butter
- 2 tablespoons olive oil
- 1 large onion, peeled and minced
- 3 large cloves garlic, peeled and minced
- 1½ cups dry white wine
- 1 cup clam juice

For the pasta

- 1 rounded tablespoon salt
- 1½ pounds spaghetti
- 1 pint (2 cups) fresh or defrosted chopped clams, with their liquid
- ½ cup fresh parsley, leaves only, chopped

   Freshly ground black pepper

- 1 tablespoon butter (optional)

   Freshly grated Parmesan cheese for serving

To make the sauce: Heat the butter and oil in a large sauté pan set over moderate heat. When the butter has melted, add the onion and cook until translucent, stirring or shaking the pan occasionally. Add the garlic and continue cooking, stirring frequently, for another 3 to 4 minutes without allowing the garlic to brown. Add the wine, clam juice, and any juice from the fresh clams, and simmer on high heat, stirring occasionally, until the mixture is reduced to about 1 cup. Keep the sauce warm while you prepare the spaghetti.

To assemble the pasta: Bring a large pot of water to a rapid boil. Add the salt. Cook the spaghetti to the desired consistency. Just before the spaghetti is ready, heat the sauce over high heat. When it comes to a simmer, add the clams and stir to coat them in the sauce. Cook for 2 to 3 minutes, stirring constantly, until the clams turn white and lose their translucent appearance. Overcooking will make them tough. Remove the pan from the heat and toss with the parsley and pepper to taste. For a richer taste, add the tablespoon of butter at this point, if desired.

Drain the pasta and divide it among 4 plates. Add the sauce and serve immediately, passing the cheese on the side.

White Clam Pizza

Makes two 14-inch thick-crust pizzas, or two 16-inch thin-crust pizzas

You can use storebought pizza dough or make your own as the base for this recipe. Making your own has never been easier, thanks to bread machines, food processors, and electric mixers that come with dough hooks. Of course, you can still make excellent pizza dough using your two hands.

For the dough

4 cups unbleached all-purpose flour

1½ teaspoons salt

¼ cup cornmeal

1 tablespoon active dry yeast

⅓ cup olive oil

1 cup plus 2 to 4 tablespoons water

For the topping

¼ cup (½ stick) butter

2 shallots, peeled and minced

2 large cloves garlic, peeled and minced

1 pint (2 cups) chopped clams, drained

⅓ cup chopped fresh flat-leaf (Italian) parsley

Freshly ground black pepper

Olive oil for brushing

½ cup freshly grated Parmesan cheese

To make the dough in a bread machine: Add all the dough ingredients, reserving ¼ cup of the water, to the bread machine, and program it for dough mode. Check the dough during the first knead cycle and add more water if necessary to form a very soft, supple ball. It's better to have the dough on the wet side rather than the dry side. At the end of the final rise, gently deflate the dough, and place it on a lightly floured work surface.

To make the dough with a mixer or food processor: Using a stand mixer fitted with the dough hook or a food processor fitted with the plastic blade, add the flour, salt, cornmeal, and yeast to the bowl. With the mixer on low or the processor motor running, add the oil and then the water until a soft, supple ball of dough begins to form. It's better to have the dough on the wet side rather than the dry side. Knead the dough in the mixer for 5 to 6 minutes, or process it for 90 seconds. Allow the dough to rest, covered, for 10 minutes, then knead it in the mixer for another 3 minutes, or process it for another minute. Allow the dough to rise in a warm place (at least 70°F) until doubled in bulk.

To make the dough by hand: Place the flour, salt, cornmeal, and yeast in a large mixing bowl. Add the oil and water and begin to knead the dough in the bowl until it forms a rough ball. Empty the dough onto a very lightly floured work surface and knead, adding more flour or water if necessary, until a very soft, smooth ball is formed (about 15 minutes). Cover the dough and allow it to rest for 10 minutes. Knead for another 5 minutes, then cover and allow the dough to rise in a warm place (at least 70°F) until doubled in bulk.

To make the topping and assemble the pizza: Heat the butter in a sauté pan set over moderate heat. Add the shallots and cook, stirring frequently, for 4 to 5 minutes, or until they are soft. Add the garlic and cook, stirring constantly to prevent burning, for another 2 minutes. Off the heat, toss the shallots and garlic together with the clams and parsley. Season with several grinds of black pepper.

Preheat the oven to 450°F, with the rack in the center position.

To make thick-crust pizzas: Roll the pizza dough out into two 14-inch circles and slide them onto lightly oiled pizza pans or a heated pizza stone sprinkled with cornmeal. Brush the top lightly with olive oil, and allow the dough to rise until puffy. Place the pizza *without the topping* in the oven, and let it bake for 6 to 7 minutes, or until the edges are dry. This prevents it from getting soggy after you add the topping. Distribute the topping evenly over the dough and sprinkle with the grated cheese. Bake for 18 to 20 minutes, or until the underside is brown and the cheese is melted and turning golden brown. Serve hot. If the top is browning before the crust is cooked through, reduce the oven temperature to 350°F and place a piece of aluminum foil lightly over the top.

To make thin-crust pizzas: Apply a light coat of olive oil to the underside of 1 large or 2 smaller heavy-duty rimmed baking sheets (jelly-roll or half sheet pans). Roll the dough out directly on the underside of the pan in a free-form shape, trying to get it as thin as possible without tearing it. Brush the top lightly with olive oil and place it (without the topping) in the oven and let it bake for 5 minutes, or just until the edges look dry. Apply the topping with a light hand (too much and the pizza will be soggy), add the cheese, and return the pizza to the oven. Bake for another 10 to 12 minutes, or until the top and underside are both well browned.

6 desserts

And now for a chapter that really needs no introduction. I think I can list on the fingers of one hand the people I know who don't eat dessert. My friends are the kinds who look at the dessert section of a menu before they even think about their main course. In our house, "What's for dessert?" is asked more often than "What's for dinner?"

Coming to Cape Cod year-round affords me the opportunity to make four seasons of desserts, leaning toward fruit tarts, ice cream, and pick-up treats that can be packed to go to the beach during the spring and warm summer months. In October and November I often make fruit pies and cobblers to take advantage of the local fall harvest. Deep winter on the Cape finds people hunkering down. They venture outside, willing to brave the bitter winds that can blow spray right up onto the road, when prompted by the promise of something good to eat. Bundled up in parkas, wool hats, and mittens, they head toward neighbors' homes for potluck suppers lit by the warmth of fireplaces and welcome company. I save complicated or richer things for the winter months, when I don't mind having the oven on and when the short days and cold weather make me think of chocolate, which makes everyone happy.

Fresh Raspberry Blueberry Tart with a Shortbread Crust

Makes one 12-inch tart

A free-form shortbread crust is easy to make and a perfect place to start if you are either new to or afraid of pastry. It makes a sturdy yet tender base for the fresh fruit topping. If you need to transport the tart before serving it, consider bringing the components (baked crust, mascarpone, and berries) separately and assembling it at the last minute.

The crust can be made up to a week ahead. Wrap it airtight in foil and store at room temperature.

For the crust

2¼ cups plus 2 tablespoons all-purpose flour

Pinch of salt

½ cup (firmly packed) light brown sugar

1 cup (2 sticks) cold unsalted butter, cut into tablespoon-sized slices

2 teaspoons almond extract

3 to 4 tablespoons water

For the mascarpone filling

8 ounces mascarpone

3 tablespoons confectioners' sugar

Finely grated zest of 1 lemon

For the topping

1 pint fresh blueberries, rinsed and gently tossed in a fine-mesh strainer to remove excess water

1 pint fresh raspberries, rinsed only if necessary and drained in a strainer

Confectioners' sugar for dusting

To make the crust: Preheat the oven to 350°F, with the rack in the center position. Line a heavy-duty baking sheet with foil (see box). Place the flour, salt, and brown sugar in the bowl of a food processor fitted with the metal blade. Pulse a few times to mix. Add the butter and almond extract to the work bowl and process for about 30 seconds, adding just enough water to make a soft dough. Gather the dough into a ball and place it on the baking sheet. Dust lightly with flour, then cover with a sheet of plastic wrap. Use the palms of your hands to press it into a 12-inch disk, with the edges slightly higher than the center (to contain the filling). Bake for 30 to 35 minutes, or until lightly browned. Allow the crust to cool on a wire rack before filling.

To fill the tart: Mix the mascarpone, 3 tablespoons of the confectioners' sugar, and the zest in a small bowl just to combine. Spread over the cooled crust. Scatter the berries over the filling, and just before serving dust with confectioners' sugar.

This is a free-form tart. If you want the crust to be a precise circle, line a 12-inch springform pan with foil and press the dough into the bottom.

155

Sand Dollars

Makes 24 to 30 pieces

There is nothing nicer than a homemade present, and when that present is something to eat it's even better. And when that something to eat is chocolate—well, do I have to say more? Inspired by the flat, silver dollar–sized shell-like creatures that you can find in tide pools and on the beach, these flat disks of chocolate are embedded with nuts and dried fruit. Once you start eating them you won't be able to stop.

Although it sometimes takes a bit of practice and patience to temper chocolate, the result is worth the effort. Even if the chocolate isn't in perfect temper (meaning that it may have some light streaks of cocoa butter on the surface) the topping will hide any imperfections.

A total 1½ to 2 cups of any combination of the following:

Slivered almonds

Coarsely chopped toasted pecans

Coarsely chopped toasted hazelnuts

Coarsely chopped toasted walnuts

Crystallized ginger, cut into ¼-inch dice

Dried cherries (sweet or sour or a combination of both)

Dried cranberries

Raisins

Dried mango, cut into ¼-inch dice

Dried apple slices, cut into ¼-inch dice

10 ounces best-quality bittersweet or semisweet chocolate, finely chopped

Place the combination of toppings you have selected in a mixing bowl and toss to combine.

Line several baking sheets with aluminum foil or parchment. Melt and temper the chocolate according to the following directions. Pour and scrape the tempered chocolate into a heavy-duty reclosable plastic bag. Seal the bag, pushing out any air, and use a pair of scissors to snip off one of the bottom corners. Make sure to cut a very small opening—you can always make it larger. Hold the bag over the lined baking sheets and pipe out a 1½- to 2-tablespoon disk of chocolate measuring 3 to 4 inches, depending on how big you want the sand dollars to be. Leave enough room between them to allow you to use a flat spatula to flatten the disks so that they are of even thickness, if necessary. While the chocolate is still semiliquid, sprinkle a very generous amount of the topping over the entire surface, pressing it in gently with your fingers or a rubber spatula. Allow the sand dollars to harden at room temperature; then peel them off the parchment or foil and store in a covered container, with waxed paper between the layers, at room temperature for up to 1 month.

To Temper Chocolate: You will need an instant-read thermometer.

If using bars: Chop the chocolate into fine pieces, and place two-thirds of it in either a double boiler or a metal bowl set over a pan of hot but not simmering water. Don't let the water in the pan touch the bottom of the bowl. Place an instant-read thermometer in the bowl with the chocolate. Stir the chocolate with a rubber spatula until the chocolate is smooth. Do not allow the temperature of the chocolate to exceed 120°F. Remove the bowl from the pan, wipe the bottom dry to prevent any water getting into the chocolate, and add the reserved chocolate to the melted chocolate, a third at a time, stirring slowly to let the chocolate melt before adding more. What you are doing here is adding some tempered chocolate to the mix while cooling down the melted chocolate. Dip your finger into the melted chocolate and smear a little bit on your upper lip. When it feels exactly body temperature, it's ready to use.

If using chocolate chips: Follow the directions given above, reserving 2 tablespoons of the chips to add to the melted chocolate. Stir and test as instructed above.

Chocolate-Covered Cape Cod Potato Chips

Makes between 50 and 75, depending on the size of the potato chips

I love the taste of sweet and salt. I think of it when I walk down most any street near the sea on the Cape in the springtime and smell the roses mingling with the smell of the ocean. Think of saltines smeared with jam or popcorn chased with a Junior Mint (my favorite movie-food combination) and you'll know what I mean. When I first saw a chocolate-covered potato chip, I thought, "You're so ugly, you'd better taste good." Boy, do they! I became an instant convert, and I bet you will as well.

Cape Cod Russet or Thick Cut Potato Chips are the perfect brand to use when making these, as they are slightly thicker (and thus sturdier and less apt to break during the dipping process), and I think the taste is first class. Thankfully, they are available nationwide, so you don't have to hop in the car and drive to the Cape in order to make these.

This is the perfect child-centered activity (preferably undertaken in a shady spot on a cool day outdoors) that appeals to adults as well. The secrets to success are to (1) not let the kids crush the bag of chips on the way home from the store, and (2) take care when melting the chocolate.

Melted chocolate is a tricky ingredient to use on its own (as opposed to mixing with butter or cream). If it isn't melted at just the right temperature, it can take a very long time to harden or can harden with white streaks showing in it. The white streaks are simply the cocoa butter in the chocolate that hasn't stayed in "temper," or properly mixed. This problem, particularly in this recipe, is merely cosmetic, so try not to worry about it if it happens to you. While the taste of premium chocolate bars is better than that of most chocolate chips, you'll probably have more luck with the chips, since they tend to be easier to melt without the angst of bars. Directions for using both follow, so the choice is yours.

Whatever you do, don't be tempted to refrigerate the dipped chips to expedite the hardening process—unless, that is, you like soggy chips.

1   5.5-ounce bag Cape Cod Potato Chips (Russet or
    Thick Cut)

9   ounces bittersweet or semisweet chocolate,
    or 9 ounces bittersweet or semisweet
    chocolate chips

Line several baking sheets with aluminum foil or parchment.

To melt chocolate bars: Chop the chocolate into fine pieces, and place two thirds of it in either a double boiler or a metal bowl set over a pan of hot but not simmering water. Don't let the water in the pan touch the bottom of the bowl. Place an instant-read thermometer in the bowl with the chocolate. Stir the chocolate with a rubber spatula until the chocolate is smooth. Do not allow the temperature of the chocolate to exceed 120°F. Remove the bowl from the pan, wipe the bottom dry to prevent any water getting into the chocolate, and add the reserved chocolate to the melted chocolate, a third at a time, stirring slowly to let the chocolate melt before adding more. What you are doing here is adding some tempered chocolate to the mix while cooling down the melted chocolate. The chocolate will begin to thicken slightly. Dip your finger into the melted chocolate and smear a little bit on your upper lip. When it feels exactly body temperature, it's ready to use.

To melt chocolate chips: Follow the directions given above, reserving 2 tablespoons of the chips to add to the melted chocolate. Stir and test as instructed above.

To dip the chips: Grasp the chip at the edge between your thumb and forefinger and gently drag it through the chocolate, covering ¾ of the chip on both sides. Some people prefer to coat only one side – it's up to you. Hold the chip over the bowl and allow any excess chocolate to drip off. Use a teaspoon or small rubber spatula to smear more onto places that you might have missed. As you coat each chip, place it on the covered baking sheet until the chocolate sets.

These probably won't last long enough to pack up to save for later, but if you do have some left over, place them in an airtight container, where they will keep for several days.

Chocolate Mint Brownies

Makes 16

A picnic on the beach, on the boat, or beside the bike path isn't complete without some sort of gooey chocolate dessert that you can eat with your fingers. Add the sparkle of mint to chocolate and you've got a treat worth including in your outdoor feast. Of course, you don't have to wait for a picnic to have an excuse to make these fudgy squares; use them as the base of a brownie ice cream sundae (facing page), or just indulge when the chocolate spirit moves you.

For the brownies

4	ounces unsweetened chocolate, chopped
½	cup (1 stick) unsalted butter
1¼	cups granulated sugar
1½	teaspoons peppermint extract
¾	teaspoon pure vanilla extract
¼	teaspoon salt
3	eggs
¾	cup all-purpose flour

For the icing

1	cup confectioners' sugar, sifted if necessary to remove any lumps
3	tablespoons unsalted butter, at room temperature
1	tablespoon milk, or as needed
2	teaspoons peppermint extract
	Green food coloring (optional)

To make the brownies: Preheat the oven to 325°F, with the rack in the center position. Line an 8-inch square baking pan with aluminum foil.

Combine the chocolate and butter in a large, heavy saucepan over low heat. Stir until melted and smooth. Let cool slightly. Use a wooden spoon to mix the sugar, peppermint extract, vanilla extract, and salt into the chocolate mixture. Beat in the eggs, one at a time, mixing well after each addition, then continue to beat until the mixture is velvety. Add the flour and mix just until blended. Pour the batter into the prepared pan.

Bake until the top is shiny and a cake tester or toothpick inserted in the center comes out with a few moist crumbs attached, 35 to 40 minutes. Let the brownies cool in the pan on a wire rack. It's better to underbake than to overbake these.

To make the icing: Combine the confectioners' sugar, butter, 1 tablespoon milk, and peppermint extract in a mixing bowl. Whisk until smooth, thinning with more milk if necessary (the icing should be thick). Stir in a drop or two of green food coloring, if desired.

To ice the brownies: Using the foil, lift the sheet of brownies from the pan and place it on a work surface. Peel back the foil sides. Spread the icing over the cooled brownies and allow it to set for 15 minutes before cutting the iced sheet into 4 equal strips and then cutting 4 strips on the adjacent side to make 16 squares. Use a metal spatula to remove the brownies from the foil. Wrap individually in plastic wrap and store in the refrigerator for up to 3 days.

Mint Chip Brownie Ice Cream Sundae

Serves 2

2 Chocolate Mint Brownies (facing page)

1 pint mint chocolate chip ice cream

Hot fudge sauce

Whipped cream

Peppermint schnapps (optional)

Place the brownies in shallow bowls. Place one or two scoops of ice cream on top and cover with hot fudge sauce. Garnish with a generous amount of whipped cream. If you really want to go overboard, drizzle some peppermint schnapps over the whipped cream.

Dune Cookies

Makes about 4 dozen cookies

At the end of a summer writing course, my teacher, Cynthia Huntington, presented me with an extraordinary gift. She invited me on a scorching, cloudless, noonday walk to one of Provincetown's most remote dune shacks to meet Annie Dillard.

"You have to promise not to gush," warned Cynthia. "She doesn't like that sort of thing." Practically speechless at my good fortune, I hoped at best to remember my name when we were introduced.

Stuffed in my day pack, along with sunscreen and a bottle of soon to be very warm water, were a paperback copy of *Pilgrim at Tinker Creek* and a plastic container full of cookies. Since I had but one evening's notice to bake something to bring, I had to "shop" in my cabinets for ingredients to go into the only means I had to express my admiration and thrill at meeting one of my very favorite authors. An extravagant amount of bittersweet chocolate chunks and toasted macadamia nuts, barely held together with a soft chocolate cookie dough, were what I came up with. It was a heavenly day—and I only gushed a little bit.

This is the perfect beach cookie; the challenge is to make enough to keep everyone happy. I like to wrap each one in foil before packing them into a picnic basket. Speaking of melt, there's nothing on earth better than a Dune Cookie that has sat in the sun for a few minutes (still wrapped in foil) to allow it to melt just a bit. The cookie oozes warm puddles of chocolate that are punctuated with the soft crunch of nuts—heaven!

16	ounces best-quality bittersweet chocolate, 8 ounces chopped, 8 ounces cut into ½-inch chunks
2	tablespoons unsalted butter
3	tablespoons all-purpose flour
¼	teaspoon baking powder
	Pinch of salt
2	extra-large eggs
⅔	cup granulated sugar
2	teaspoons pure vanilla extract
8	ounces unsalted macadamia nuts

Preheat the oven to 350°F, with the rack in the center position. Line 2 heavy-duty baking sheets with parchment or foil. Melt the chopped chocolate together with the butter in a double-boiler or in a small bowl in a microwave oven and allow it to cool slightly.

Sift the flour, baking powder, and salt together into a small bowl. In the bowl of an electric mixer, beat the eggs, sugar, and vanilla on high speed until the mixture is thick and light in color. On low speed, add the melted chocolate and flour, mixing only to incorporate them. Mix in the nuts and chocolate chunks.

Use a tablespoon to drop rounded mounds of batter onto the baking sheets, about 1 inch apart—these don't spread very much.

Bake for 12 minutes, or until the tops look shiny and slightly cracked. They will be very wet in the center. Do not remove the cookies from the baking sheets until they have thoroughly cooled.

Quick and Easy Rocky Road Fudge

Makes 1¼ pounds, or 24 generous pieces

The crowd starts gathering even before Provincetown fudge maestro Paul Endich unlocks the door to The Penny Patch. By the time he has lit the flame under the giant copper pot, has the sugar syrup at a rolling boil, and is consulting the thermometer to see if it's time to add the butter and chocolate, Commercial Street traffic (typically slow at best) has practically ground to a halt. Faces press expectantly against the glass storefront where "Fudge" is exclaimed in big pink letters. Noses sniff wildly at the intoxicating aroma emanating from the open door. The line starts at the fudge counter and backs all the way out to the street.

Ah, the agonizing choices: chocolate with or without nuts, penuche, maple, peanut butter, rocky road. "What the heck," is the almost universal conclusion, "I'll take one of each!" How many times a day do Paul and his daughter Tamara hear this as they prepare to stuff yet another square of heaven into a pristine tissue paper–lined box? "Enough to make us happy to be here," says Paul.

Paul's recipe for fudge requires a fine hand, a keen eye, and lots of experience. This "home kitchen" recipe may lack the professional touch, but the results are foolproof.

1⅔   cups granulated sugar

⅔   cup evaporated milk

2   ounces unsweetened chocolate, chopped

1½   cups miniature marshmallows

¾   cup toasted nuts of your choice, coarsely chopped

6   ounces semisweet chocolate chips

Coat the bottom and sides of an 8-by-8-inch pan with unsalted butter and then line it with foil, allowing the ends to overlap the rim of the pan. Coat the bottom and sides of the foil with more butter.

Add the sugar and evaporated milk to a heavy-bottomed 1½-quart saucepan set over medium heat. Stir constantly with a wooden spoon until the sugar dissolves and the mixture begins to simmer. Allow the mixture to come to a slow boil and cook it for 5 minutes, stirring constantly. Remember to scrape the sides and bottom of the pan so the mixture doesn't burn.

Remove the pan from the heat and stir in the unsweetened chocolate, stirring until it melts. Stir in the marshmallows and nuts and continue to stir until the fudge begins to cool and thicken. Stir in the chocolate chips and pour and scrape the mixture into the prepared pan. Allow the fudge to sit at room temperature until firm.

Turn the fudge out onto a cutting board and use a long, sharp knife dipped in hot water and wiped dry to cut it into squares.

The fudge can be stored in an airtight container at room temperature for several weeks.

You can use any flavor chips in this recipe, such as white chocolate, peanut butter, or mint chocolate.

↔ ⊹ ↔

Toasting the nuts ahead of time brings out their flavor. Sprinkle them in one layer on a heavy-duty baking sheet and bake in a 350°F oven for 10 to 12 minutes, or until they just start to brown. Use a wide metal spatula to turn them, and bake for another 3 to 4 minutes. Cool the nuts to room temperature on the baking sheet before using or storing in a heavy-duty freezer-strength reclosable plastic bag.

Lavender Crème Brûlée
Chester Restaurant

Serves 6

"So, where's your favorite place to eat in Provincetown?" is a frequently asked question. People stop me on the street to ask, friends coming for vacation ask, people writing food and travel stories ask, locals ask. Of course, the answer depends on your budget and on whether you are looking for "from the beach" casual or "grown-up" dining (read: leave the kids with a sitter).

If you are looking for divine food in a magical yet totally relaxed setting, if you want to feel completely welcome by restaurateurs who understand what world-class dining is all about, then look no further than the white-columned Greek Revival building that houses Chester Restaurant, where John Guerra and Jay Coburn have created *the* place to eat in town.

It was hard to choose which special recipe to include from the dozens that appear each season on the ever-evolving menu at Chester. This very special crème brûlée with its lavender-perfumed custard and burnt sugar topping will transport you to the south of France, while keeping Cape Cod Bay practically within view.

For the custard

2   cups (1 pint) heavy cream
2   tablespoons dried lavender, or ¼ cup fresh lavender leaves, finely chopped
1   teaspoon pure vanilla extract
     Pinch of salt
8   large egg yolks
⅓   cup granulated sugar

For the topping

½   cup granulated sugar

To make the custard: Add the cream, lavender, vanilla, and salt to a heavy-bottomed 2-quart saucepan set over moderate heat. Stir occasionally with a wooden spoon or whisk. When the mixture begins to simmer (tiny bubbles will form around the edge of the pan), remove the pan from the heat and let the mixture sit at room temperature for at least 1 hour to allow the flavor of the lavender to steep into the cream. Or, to extract the maximum flavor, cool the mixture to room temperature, cover, and refrigerate overnight.

continued on next page

Preheat the oven to 325°F, with the rack in the center position. Reheat the infused cream to a bare simmer, stirring once or twice. In a large mixing bowl, whisk together the egg yolks and sugar until light yellow and slightly thickened. Pour in the hot cream, whisking to mix completely. Strain the custard through a fine sieve into a large measuring cup or spouted pitcher, and skim off any bubbles.

Fill six 8-ounce ramekins or brûlée dishes almost to the top with the custard, and place them in a shallow roasting pan or heavy-duty rimmed baking sheet, so that the edges are not touching. Add hot water to come halfway up the sides of the ramekins. Cover the pan loosely with foil and bake for 35 to 45 minutes (depending on the density of the ramekin or dish), or until the custards are set up and the tip of a sharp knife inserted in the center comes out clean.

Transfer the ramekins to a wire rack to cool to room temperature, then refrigerate, uncovered, to cool completely.

To make the topping: At least 30 minutes before serving, sprinkle the top of each custard with a generous amount of sugar. Using a kitchen blowtorch (available from a hardware or kitchenware store), melt the sugar by moving the flame slowly back and forth over the surface until the sugar bubbles and has liquefied. Return the brûlées to the refrigerator to allow the topping to harden (about 15 minutes).

Jay says he doesn't recommend using a broiler to melt the sugar topping—it warms the custard too much and makes it runny.

Mixed Berry Shortcake

Serves 9

Plump berries, bursting with sun-ripened flavor, perfectly balance the melt-in-your-mouth tender flakiness of homemade biscuits in this heirloom recipe. Topped with a generous dollop of freshly whipped heavy cream, this classic dessert can be made to feed two or twenty.

For the biscuits

¾	cup whole milk
1	tablespoon white vinegar
½	cup (1 stick) unsalted butter, cut into pieces
2	cups all-purpose flour
2	teaspoons baking powder
½	teaspoon baking soda
½	teaspoon salt
2	tablespoons granulated sugar

For the topping

1	quart (4 cups) mixed berries, such as strawberries, blueberries, raspberries, and blackberries
⅓	cup granulated sugar
2	cups (1 pint) heavy cream, very cold

To make the biscuits: Preheat the oven to 425°F, with the rack in the center position. Line a heavy-duty baking sheet with foil or parchment. Measure the milk in a 1-cup measure, then stir in the vinegar. The mixture will curdle. Set aside.

Place the butter in a medium-sized mixing bowl, then set a wire strainer over the bowl. Add the flour, baking powder, baking soda, salt, and sugar to the strainer and shake the dry ingredients into the bowl over the butter. Use 2 butter knives in a crisscross motion to cut the flour into the butter until the mixture resembles coarse crumbs. Dribble in the milk while using a fork to mix the dough until it is sticky and just starts to hold together. It will not be a smooth ball. Turn the dough out onto a lightly floured work surface and, using your hands and a dough scraper, gently knead the dough about 10 turns into a smooth ball. Pat the dough into a 9-inch rectangle about ½ inch thick. Use a straight, sharp knife to cut the dough into 3 equal strips, then cut each strip in thirds to make 9 biscuits. Place the biscuits 1½ inches apart on the prepared baking sheet and bake for 14 to 16 minutes, or until the tops are lightly browned. Remove to a wire rack to cool.

To assemble the shortcakes: Rinse the strawberries and slice them. Combine the berries in a mixing bowl, sprinkle with the sugar, and set aside. In a chilled bowl with chilled beaters, whip the cream until it holds soft peaks. Slice the biscuits in half, and place the bottom half of each biscuit in an individual shallow bowl or rimmed dish. Spoon some berries and juice onto the biscuit half. Place the top of each biscuit on the fruit and add a generous dollop of whipped cream. Serve immediately.

Pumpkin Cheesecake

Serves 10

With its beautiful color and creamy-smooth filling, fragrant with cinnamon, ginger, and nutmeg, this cheesecake is the perfect Thanksgiving dessert. None of your guests will ever know how easy this was to make, or that you made it weeks ahead and froze it. But don't save it only for Thanksgiving—it's the perfect, easy-to-make dessert for any time of year.

2   8-ounce packages regular cream cheese (not whipped, low-fat, or nonfat), at room temperature

½   cup granulated sugar

2   extra-large eggs

½   teaspoon ground nutmeg

½   teaspoon ground cinnamon

½   teaspoon ground ginger

1   cup canned pumpkin purée (not pumpkin pie filling)

1   9-inch chocolate crumb crust, homemade (facing page) or storebought

Preheat the oven to 350°F, with the rack in the center position. Place the cream cheese and sugar in a medium-sized mixing bowl, and use a hand-held mixer on medium speed to mix until smooth. Add the eggs, nutmeg, cinnamon, ginger, and pumpkin and mix until well combined, scraping the sides of the bowl with a rubber spatula as necessary. Pour and scrape the mixture into the crust and bake for 30 minutes, or until the top looks dry except for a quarter-sized spot in the very center. Cool on a rack at room temperature for 30 minutes, then either leave the cheesecake at room temperature for up to 6 hours before serving, cover with plastic wrap and refrigerate for up to 3 days, or wrap in several layers of plastic wrap and then in foil and freeze for up to 2 months. Defrost at room temperature, still wrapped.

Chocolate Crumb Crust

Makes one 9-inch pie crust

Look for Famous Chocolate Wafers in the cookie section of the supermarket.

1   package (7 ounces) Nabisco Famous Chocolate Wafers, each broken into several pieces

¼   cup granulated sugar

6   tablespoons unsalted butter, melted and slightly cooled

Preheat the oven to 450°F, with the rack in the center position. Butter or use nonstick cooking spray to coat a 9-inch pie pan. Pulverize the cookies in a food processor fitted with the metal blade, or place them in a freezer-strength reclosable plastic bag and crush them by rolling over them with a heavy rolling pin or by gently banging them with the bottom of a saucepan until the mixture is fine crumbs.

In a medium-sized mixing bowl, combine the crumbs, sugar, and butter. Use a fork to toss the mixture to combine the ingredients. Scrape the mixture into the prepared pie pan and use your fingers to press the crumbs evenly into the bottom and up the sides. Don't worry about making the sides perfectly even.

Bake the crust for 5 minutes, and cool before using.

Cranberry-Pear Linzertorte

Serves 8 to 10

Alice Wiebusch, pastry chef at Anago in the Lenox Hotel in Boston, uses hazelnuts, cranberries, and pears to create this new take on a very classic recipe. It is the showpiece in this very special restaurant, where Alice makes her magic in the pastry kitchen. Inspired by her love of Cape Cod, and especially by the hearty flavors of fall, this gorgeous, lattice-topped tart makes a show-stopping dessert that lights up not only the table but the taste buds of everyone lucky enough to taste it.

For the crust

- 2 cups all-purpose flour
- 1 cup toasted, skinned hazelnuts (see box)
- ¾ cup granulated sugar
- 1 teaspoon baking powder
- ½ teaspoon ground cinnamon
- ¾ cup (1½ sticks) cold unsalted butter, cut into small pieces
- 2 extra-large egg yolks
- 2 teaspoons finely grated orange zest
- 1 teaspoon pure vanilla extract
- 2 tablespoons ice water

For the filling

- 1 pound fresh whole cranberries, picked over to remove any stems and moldy berries
- 4 to 5 slightly underripe Bosc pears, peeled, cored, and coarsely chopped to about the size of cranberries, to measure 4 cups
- 1 cup granulated sugar
- ⅓ cup pear nectar (available in the juice section of the supermarket)

Unsweetened whipped cream or vanilla ice cream for topping (optional)

To make the crust: Place the flour, hazelnuts, sugar, baking powder, and cinnamon in the work bowl of a food processor fitted with the metal blade. Process, pulsing the machine on and off, until the nuts are very finely ground, 15 to 20 seconds. Add the butter and pulse until the mixture is the consistency of coarse meal. Add the egg yolks, zest, vanilla, and ice water and process just until the dough comes together. Divide the dough into 2 portions so that one portion contains one-third of the dough and the second portion contains two-thirds of the dough. Form each portion into a ball, flatten (dusting with flour if necessary to keep the dough from sticking), and wrap each in plastic. Chill for at least 1 hour.

To make the filling: While the dough is chilling, combine the cranberries, pears, sugar, and pear nectar in a large saucepan over high heat. Bring the mixture to a boil, stirring until the sugar dissolves. Reduce the heat and simmer, uncovered, stirring often, until the mixture has reduced and thickened. Be sure to scrape the bottom of the pan while stirring, to prevent scorching. Remove from the heat and allow to cool to room temperature.

To toast hazelnuts: You can often find untoasted hazelnuts that have the thin, brown skin removed. This will save you the step of removing the skin yourself. They should be toasted to bring out the flavor even if they have already been skinned. Preheat the oven to 375°F, with the rack in the upper third of the oven, but not the highest position. Add the hazelnuts to a heavy-duty rimmed baking sheet or shallow roasting pan. Bake for 15 minutes, then briskly shake the pan back and forth to rotate the nuts. Bake for another 10 minutes or so, until the nuts are light golden brown. They will not toast evenly, but try to avoid creating any burned spots. If the hazelnuts are already skinned, let them cool in the pan. If they have the skins on, empty the hot nuts onto one half of a large bath towel. Flip the other half on top and use your hands to rub the nuts briskly. Most of the skin will flake off. Don't worry about any that remains.

To assemble and bake the tart: Preheat the oven to 350°F, with the oven rack in the center position. Apply a light coating of nonstick cooking spray to the bottom and sides of a 10-inch tart pan with a removable bottom. Place the tart pan on a heavy-duty rimmed baking sheet to catch any filling that overflows. Lightly flour your fingers, and use them to press the larger portion of dough into the bottom and up the sides of the tart pan. Scrape the filling into the crust; it should just reach the top of the crust.

On a lightly floured surface, or between 2 pieces of plastic wrap, roll out the smaller portion of dough into a 12-inch by 8-inch rectangle. Use a fluted pastry cutter or a small knife to cut the dough into ten ¾-inch-wide strips. Use the strips to weave a lattice crust over the top of the tart by crisscrossing the strips over one another. Anchor the strips to the dough on the edges of the tart by pinching the strips against the edges. Bake until the filling bubbles slightly and the crust is golden, 45 to 50 minutes. Cool on a wire rack before removing the tart from the pan. Cut the tart into wedges and serve topped with whipped cream or a scoop of vanilla ice cream, if desired.

7 drinks

Think outside the box and offer your guests something beyond beer or chardonnay to quench a summer day's thirst. A tall glass of iced Sun Tea garnished with a sprig of fresh mint, or a Cranberry Martini can make cocktail hour on your deck *the* place to be.

A Medley of Libations

If you are looking beyond a glass of chilled white wine for something
to kick off the cocktail hour or put some extra
spice into brunch, consider one of these Cape classics.

Sea Breeze

Serves 1

The color alone makes this a jewel among mixed drinks.

1½ ounces vodka

2 ounces grapefruit juice

3 ounces cranberry juice

   Ice

1 lime wedge for garnish

Pour the vodka, grapefruit, and cranberry juice into a highball glass filled with ice. Stir well and garnish with the lime wedge.

Red Snapper

Serves 1

One Cape Cod version of a Bloody Mary.

2 ounces gin

4 ounces spicy tomato juice, chilled

¼ teaspoon celery salt

   Freshly ground black pepper

2 to 3 dashes Worcestershire sauce

2 to 3 drops Tabasco sauce

1 tablespoon lime juice

   Ice

1 stalk celery from the heart of the celery, leaves intact, for garnish

Add the gin, tomato juice, celery salt, pepper to taste, Worcestershire sauce, Tabasco sauce, and lime juice to a highball glass filled with ice. Stir to combine and garnish by inserting the celery stalk into the glass.

Red Tide

Serves 1

A clam's-eye view of a Bloody Mary.

- 2   ounces vodka
- 1   cup Clamato juice (available in the juice section of the supermarket), chilled (see box)
- 1   tablespoon lemon juice
- 1   teaspoon Worcestershire sauce
- 1/2   teaspoon prepared horseradish
     Pinch of freshly ground black pepper
- 1/4   teaspoon celery salt
- 2   or 3 drops Tabasco sauce
     Ice
- 1   cooked, shelled, chilled shrimp for garnish

Add the vodka, Clamato juice, lemon juice, Worcestershire sauce, horseradish, pepper, celery salt, and Tabasco sauce to a highball glass filled with ice. Stir to combine and garnish with the shrimp affixed to the top of a wooden skewer or long toothpick.

If you can't find Clamato juice, use ¾ cup spicy tomato juice and ¼ cup clam juice.

Mulled Cider

Serves 8

I use my slow cooker in every season—to avoid using the oven in warm weather, to make oatmeal overnight without ever having to stir the pot, and to make hot mulled cider when there is a nip in the air. The welcome fragrance of cinnamon and cloves, accented with orange, lemon, and ginger, will waft through your kitchen and into the hearts of everyone within nose reach. If you don't have a slow cooker, you can make this in a pan as well—instructions for both methods follow.

I use hard cider and apple brandy to make this very adult drink. You can certainly substitute regular apple cider and leave out the apple brandy if you are serving children.

8 cups hard apple cider (see box)

1 cup apple brandy (Calvados or applejack)

2 cinnamon sticks

12 whole cloves, tied in cheesecloth

⅔ cup honey

1 tablespoon peeled and finely grated fresh ginger (see box)

1 cup dried apple slices, cut into ¼-inch pieces (see box)

1 navel orange, cut in half and then into ½-inch slices

1 large lemon, cut into ¼-inch slices, seeds removed

Place all of the ingredients in a slow cooker or in a non-reactive 2-quart heavy-bottomed pot set over low heat. If you are using a slow cooker, set it on High for 1 hour and then turn it to Low and cook for another hour. If cooking on top of the stove, bring the ingredients in the pot to a low simmer and cook, uncovered, for 30 minutes. Remove the cloves and cinnamon sticks. Serve hot by ladling into mugs or heatproof glasses.

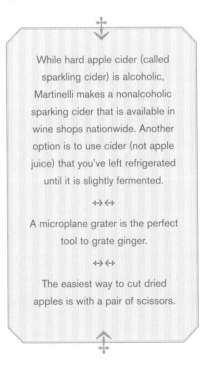

While hard apple cider (called sparkling cider) is alcoholic, Martinelli makes a nonalcoholic sparking cider that is available in wine shops nationwide. Another option is to use cider (not apple juice) that you've left refrigerated until it is slightly fermented.

A microplane grater is the perfect tool to grate ginger.

The easiest way to cut dried apples is with a pair of scissors.

Candy Manor Hot Chocolate

Serves 4 to 6

Naomi Turner is a multitalented woman, and both her dance studio and her extraordinary chocolate shop on Chatham's Main Street attest to her ability to speak to the things that can make life beautiful. Walking into the Chatham Candy Manor is, judging from the expressions of rapture on the faces of everyone in the store, an experience that anyone who loves candy—and especially chocolate—lives for. Everywhere you look, sweet things are displayed with an eye for great design and with packaging that is as eye-catching as the contents. Choosing from the dozens upon dozens of chocolate jewels in the glass cases is an almost impossible task, and watching customers sigh and point and sigh and point again is to share their agony. But of course, each bite is ecstasy.

Every Christmas season, Naomi and her partner, David Veach, continue a tradition begun by Naomi's mother, who started the business in 1955. These candy cane–making demonstrations are so popular that folks line up early to get a chance to watch. Another tradition is to provide tastes of their famous hot chocolate, which is flavored with mint and topped with candy cane–infused whipped cream.

For the peppermint whipped cream

1   cup (½ pint) heavy cream, chilled

¼   teaspoon pure vanilla extract

2   tablespoons confectioners' sugar

2   tablespoons crushed peppermint candy

For the hot chocolate

3   ounces unsweetened chocolate, grated

4   cups whole milk

⅓   cup granulated sugar

⅓   cup boiling water

1   teaspoon ground cinnamon

1   teaspoon peppermint extract

Begin by making the whipped cream: Place a 1½-quart metal bowl plus the beater for either a hand-held or stand mixer in the freezer for 30 minutes before beginning. Beat the cream with the vanilla and sugar until it forms soft peaks. Use a rubber spatula to fold in the crushed candy. Refrigerate until ready to serve.

To make the hot chocolate: Melt the chocolate in a 2½-quart mixing bowl set over, but not touching, the bottom of a pan of gently boiling water. The bowl will seem much bigger than necessary, but it will need to accommodate the milk later on. Stir once or twice with a rubber spatula. While the chocolate is melting, pour the milk into a 2-quart heavy-bottomed saucepan set over moderate heat. Whisk in the sugar and cook until the milk begins to simmer and small bubbles form around the edge of the pan.

Reduce the heat under the chocolate to a bare simmer. Add the water to the melted chocolate and beat with a stiff wire whisk or hand-held electric mixer until smooth. Dribble in the hot milk while you continue to beat. When the ingredients are incorporated, remove the bowl from the water bath and stir in the cinnamon and peppermint extract.

Serve by ladling the hot chocolate into mugs and topping with a generous dollop of the whipped cream.

Cranberry Martini

Serves 1

Marty's, the place where I buy my wine, also sells all sorts of exotic liqueurs, brandies, beers, and cordials. While perusing the shelves one day, I happened upon a bottle of cranberry liqueur. "Hey, Marty," I called over the rack of California chardonnay, "what do you use this for?" When he replied, "Cranberry martinis," I thought, Now that would be something to sip while you watch the sun set over the bay. Here's Marty's recipe.

6   dried cranberries

1½   ounces vodka, plus more if necessary

     Crushed ice

½   ounce cranberry liqueur

Place the dried cranberries in the vodka, cover, and allow to sit for 1 hour or as long as 24 hours. Pour off the vodka into a jigger or measuring cup and reserve. Add enough additional vodka to bring the amount back to 1½ ounces. Place the cranberries in a chilled martini glass.

Fill a martini shaker with crushed ice. Pour in the vodka and the cranberry liqueur. Shake well, then strain into the martini glass. Serve immediately.

Sun Tea

Makes 4 cups

A special alchemy takes place when you make this simple drink. Watching the tea infuse the liquid in the sunlight and turn it a golden amber reminds me that the simpler things are, the better they taste. This makes a very concentrated solution, which will stand up to the addition of lots of ice when served.

Sweetening iced tea (or coffee) with a simple syrup solution is a trick I learned from my New Orleans friends.

For the tea

4   cups water, at room temperature

4   teabags of your choice (I like to use Constant Comment or mint)

1   large lemon, scrubbed and thinly sliced, seeds removed if desired

Fresh mint sprigs for garnish

For the simple syrup

1   cup granulated sugar

1/3   cup water

To make the tea: Add the water to a 1^{1}/$_{2}$-quart clear glass or plastic pitcher. Add the teabags, tying the strings around the handle, if possible. If there is no handle, just allow the teabags to float in the water—you can use a slotted spoon to fish them out later. Add the lemon slices.

Place the pitcher in direct sunlight (you may want to cover the top if you do this outside). It will take 45 minutes to an hour to make the infusion.

Meanwhile, make the simple syrup: Combine the sugar and water in a small saucepan set over high heat. Stir constantly while the mixture comes to a boil. When the sugar has dissolved, remove it from the heat and allow it to cool to room temperature. Pour the simple syrup into a small pitcher.

Serve the tea in tall, ice-filled glasses garnished with fresh mint, and pass the simple syrup on the side.

8 condiments

I own a large, unlined copper confiture pan that I hauled back from Paris thinking I'd spend my idle time whipping up jams and jellies with fruit picked from my own backyard. But idle time and backyards were in short supply, so we used the pan to hold mail-order catalogues that everyone in the house meant to read . . . one day. Then it was used to store a collection of board games that were all missing a vital piece or two, and finally it held a massive collection of half-painted model cars the kids had started decorating with great enthusiasm but eventually lost interest in.

I'd forgotten about that pan until the first time we spent a whole summer on the Cape and wandered into the back-yard of our rented cottage to find the beach plums, deep purple, plump, and ripe for picking. I learned right off that I was not a jelly maker (too much precision is involved), but I was a natural at jam, which is far more forgiving. I made good use of the now battered and tarnished pan and didn't stop at beach plum jam. I became a jam maniac and soon had the shelves of our small pantry sagging under the weight of half-pint Ball jars of pear marmalade, cranberry chutney, spiced peach conserve, and homemade catsup. Once I got the system down, I was turning out so many jars that I was running out of room. When it got to the point that I was considering buying sugar in 50-pound bags, I came

to my senses and stopped for a while. My friends and neighbors were delighted with the fact that every time I stopped by it was with at least two or three jars of some-thing from my "putting by" craze.

You don't need a fancy copper pan to make great jam or jelly. Homemade condiments will spoil you, and you'll look at both the price and quality of storebought stuff with a whole new eye.

While commercially prepared tartar sauce is fine, more often than not, it's not on hand when you need it. Other recipes in this chapter guide you through the simple steps of using ingredients you most probably have on hand to make the condiments you don't.

Beach Plum Jam

Makes 6 half-pints

If you are into almost instant gratification with just a moderate amount of effort, the good news is that at 4:30 today I was picking in the dunes and now, at 6:30, I'm writing this recipe with 6 lovely jars of jam sitting on my counter.

With beach plums you get almost as much pit as you do pulp, so pick a lot. Otherwise you'll have to be satisfied with a very few jars of jam. Different types of pectin call for different ratios of fruit to sugar and have different cooking instructions. Be sure to read the package insert and figure out how much sugar and pectin you will need for the amount of cooked fruit pulp you have. In addition, be sure to sterilize the jars and tops before you start.

4   to 5 pounds beach plums

1   cup orange juice or water

Pectin of your choice

Sugar (use the amount specified in the pectin package)

Rinse the plums and place them in a large kettle. Add the orange juice or water and cook over high heat until the mixture starts to simmer. Lower the heat to medium and cook the fruit, stirring frequently to prevent burning, until the skins split. Use the back of the spoon to mash the plums up against the side of the pan to remove the pits from the pulp. Cook for 20 minutes, continuing to stir almost constantly, until the plums have dissolved into pulp.

Carefully pour the hot mixture into a large colander with holes large enough to allow the juice and pulp to pass through but small enough to contain the pits, set over a large mixing bowl. You should end up with a total of about 5 cups of juice and pulp. The amount will vary depending on how ripe and plump the fruit was.

Follow the directions for making jam on the package insert of the pectin you have selected. Spoon the hot jam into the sterilized jars, cover with the sterilized caps, and tighten the bands. The vacuum created as the jam cools will seal the lid to the jar.

Bread and Butter Pickles

Makes 4 pints

As vegetables go from the "bigger is better" craze to the miniature and heirloom phase, you can always count on pickling cukes to remain steadfastly true to form: lovely, plump, stubby, and, best of all, unwaxed. You know summer is truly here when they start arriving in markets and at farm stands. If you've always wondered how to make pickles from scratch, here's your chance. Your tuna sandwich will thank you.

You can use the combination of spices indicated here or purchase a pickling spice blend in the spice and herb section of the supermarket.

1½ pounds pickling cucumbers, scrubbed

1½ pounds Vidalia or other sweet onions, peeled, cut in half, and then cut into ¼-inch slices

3 cloves garlic, peeled and crushed (but left in one piece)

2 medium red bell peppers, cut in half, seeds removed, cored, and cut into ¼-inch dice

2 medium green bell peppers, cut in half, seeds removed, cored, and cut into ¼-inch dice

2½ tablespoons kosher or coarse salt

4 cups cider vinegar

2 cups (packed) light brown sugar

Pickling spices

2 teaspoons ground turmeric

1 tablespoon mustard seed

1½ tablespoons celery seed

2 teaspoons dill seed

2 bay leaves, crumbled (or substitute 3 tablespoons purchased pickling spice blend)

If the cucumbers have very thick skins, place them in a sieve and rinse them with several changes of boiling water, followed by a cold-water rinse. Slice the cucumbers into ½-inch-thick rounds. Place the cucumbers, onions, garlic, and bell peppers in a large glass or crockery bowl. Sprinkle with the salt and toss well. Cover with plastic wrap or a clean dish towel and allow the bowl to sit overnight or for at least 12 hours at room temperature.

Drain the liquid from the bowl and discard it. Transfer the cucumbers, onions, garlic, and bell peppers to a large sieve and rinse with cold running water.

Add the vinegar, sugar, and pickling spices to a large, nonreactive saucepan set over high heat. Bring to a rapid boil and cook, uncovered, for 10 minutes. Add the vegetables to the saucepan, return to a boil, cook for 1 minute, and remove from the heat.

Spoon the pickles and liquid into sterilized canning jars. Cover with sterilized lids and allow them to sit, refrigerated, for at least 2 days before serving.

Cocktail Sauce

Makes 1¼ cups

Don't use horseradish that's been sitting in your refrigerator for 6 months, as it will have lost its potency.

½ cup purchased catsup (or Oven-Roasted Tomato Catsup, page 204)

½ cup purchased chili sauce

¼ cup prepared horseradish, or more to taste

2 tablespoons Worcestershire sauce

3 to 4 drops Tabasco sauce, or to taste

Place all the ingredients in a small mixing bowl and stir with a fork to combine. Refrigerate for up to 2 months in a tightly covered container until ready to serve.

Tartar Sauce

Makes about 1 cup

Eating fried clams or oysters without tartar sauce is like eating birthday cake without ice cream. Some people make tartar sauce simply by combining mayonnaise and chopped pickles. This recipes goes a little beyond that.

1 cup purchased mayonnaise

3 tablespoons flat-leaf (Italian) parsley, leaves only, rinsed, dried, and minced

1 rounded tablespoon capers, drained (liquid reserved) and finely minced

1 teaspoon juice from capers

¼ cup drained, finely minced dill pickle

3 tablespoons Dijon mustard

2 or 3 drops Tabasco sauce

Salt and freshly ground black pepper

Place all the ingredients in a mixing bowl and stir with a fork to combine. Refrigerate in a tightly sealed container for up to 3 weeks.

The Green Briar Jam Kitchen

There are many special reasons to fall in love with the Green Briar Jam Kitchen, a hidden treasure tucked away on a side road off scenic Route 6 in East Sandwich. If you're a child, you can pet the bunnies or see the frogs in the Green Briar Nature Center. If you're an admirer of lovely gardens, you can wander among the beds of wild-flowers. If, like me, you grew up on stories about Peter Rabbit, Jimmy Skunk, Grandfather Frog, Johnny Chuck, Sammy Jay, and Reddy Fox, you will be enchanted to discover where naturalist and illustrator Thornton W. Burgess wrote and illustrated over 170 books and 15,000 stories beloved by generations of children in all parts of the world.

What drew me to Green Briar in the first place was the gift of a jar of sun-cooked strawberry jam. The essence of sweet strawberries grown in summer sun was captured in the unassuming glass jar with the white metal cap. The taste conjured up women in aprons picking through white enameled tins full of perfectly ripe fruit, a bank of gas burners in a line, ladles, sieves, the aroma of heavenly treats. The reality was even better than my fantasy. The robin's-egg blue and creamy white kitchen, flooded with sunlight and with a view of trees hung with bird feeders, is the "jam control center." The women, both volunteers and staff, work nonstop, scooping, measuring, weighing, stirring, skimming, and ladling the bounty of their labors into the gleaming glass jars, capping them with the white metal lids, and lowering them into the water bath for sterilization. After they are cooled, the jewel-like jars are displayed in the Jam Kitchen's shop, where tourists like me scoop them up by the dozen to take home for whenever we want a true taste of Cape Cod.

The kitchen at Green Briar holds the oldest solar cooker in operation in the United States. If you have ever grown seedlings in a cold frame, you can begin to get an idea of what these solar cookers look like. Attached to the south side of the kitchen, they are accessed through a window that slides up to reveal a rectangular box into which ripe fruit is spread. The sun cooks them for 3 days before they are spooned into glass jars for lucky tourists and locals to take home. When I asked about doing this at home, I was told that the best way would be to spread the fruit on a tray and leave it in a closed car in the sun for a couple of hot summer days. I haven't had the chance to try this yet, but I promise that someday I will. Meanwhile, here are a few simple but ever-so-delicious recipes from the Green Briar Jam Kitchen.

Strawberry Jam

Makes five 6-ounce jars

Wait for native (local) strawberries to make this jam, as they have the most flavor. Take care to rinse them very well—they are often full of grit.

3   pints ripe strawberries, hulled and rinsed

4   cups granulated sugar

Add the strawberries to a 3-quart nonreactive pan set over moderate heat. Use a potato masher to crush but not purée them. Add the sugar, mix to combine, and bring the mixture to a boil. Reduce the heat and simmer gently for 15 to 20 minutes, or until the mixture has started to thicken. Skim the foam from the surface. Spoon into sterilized jars and seal according to the manufacturer's directions.

"It's a wonderful thing to sweeten the world, which is in a jam and needs preserving."
–Thornton W. Burgess

Spiced Pear Jam

Makes five 6-ounce jars

This lovely jam sparkles with a rainbow of flavors. While it's perfect on toast and muffins, it's also great on pancakes and waffles.

3   pounds ripe, flavorful pears, cored, peeled, and cut into 1-inch pieces

Juice of 1 lemon

1   large navel orange

1   lemon

1   cup crushed canned pineapple, with juice reserved

¼   teaspoon ground nutmeg

¼   teaspoon ground cloves

1   tablespoon peeled and chopped ginger

4   cups granulated sugar

Add the pears to a mixing bowl and toss with the lemon juice. Cut the ends from the orange and lemon. Cut them in half. Then cut each half lengthwise into 3 wedges. Remove any seeds. Slice each wedge crosswise into thin slices. Add the orange, lemon, and pineapple and its juice to a 3-quart nonreactive pan set over medium-low heat. Bring to a simmer and cook, stirring frequently, over low heat until the lemon and orange are tender, about 20 minutes. Add the pears, spices, ginger, and sugar and continue to cook over low heat, stirring frequently, until the mixture is slightly thickened, about 20 minutes. Spoon into sterilized jars and seal according to the manufacturer's directions.

Cranberry Salsa

Makes about 3 cups

If you are looking for something slightly nontraditional to serve with turkey or chicken or even steak, look no further than this marvelously flavorful cooked salsa. With its vibrant colors and chile pepper warmth, it makes a great condiment. You can use it in sandwiches as well.

- 1   pound fresh or frozen cranberries (if frozen, no need to defrost)
- 1   medium onion, peeled and coarsely chopped
- 2   cloves garlic, peeled and minced
- 1   large navel orange, zest removed and cut into long, thin strips, pulp chopped
- 1⅓ cups (packed) dark brown sugar
- 1   tablespoon minced red chile pepper
- ⅓   cup Triple Sec or other orange liqueur, or orange juice
- 1   cup orange juice

Place all the ingredients in a 2-quart nonreactive pan set over medium heat. Cover and bring to a boil, then lower the heat and cook for 15 minutes, stirring once or twice, until the cranberries are soft but not disintegrated. Serve hot, warm, or at room temperature. This salsa will keep in a covered container in the refrigerator for 1 month.

Lobster Butter

Makes about 1 cup

Although regular butter is great for dipping succulent bits of lobster meat, you can gild the lily further by saving shells from a previous lobster dinner and making lobster butter. While using this butter may constitute "double dipping," I say that nothing exceeds and succeeds (in this case) like excess.

This butter can be frozen up to 6 months, stored in a tightly sealed container.

        Shell and body of one 1½-pound lobster
1   cup (2 sticks) unsalted butter
1   bay leaf
8   whole peppercorns
2   large sprigs fresh thyme, left whole

Use a cleaver or heavy chef's knife to cut the shell and body into 2- to 3-inch pieces. Place them, a few at a time, in a food processor fitted with the metal blade and process until they are crushed—they don't all have to be the same size.

Melt the butter in a 2-quart saucepan set over moderate heat. Add the shells and cook, stirring continuously, for 10 minutes. Add the bay leaf, peppercorns, and thyme, and then add enough water just to cover. Place a lid on the pan and simmer over medium-low heat for 30 minutes.

Strain the liquid through a fine-mesh strainer lined with several thicknesses of cheesecloth, pressing the solids to extract as much liquid as possible. Pour into a small bowl, cover, and refrigerate. When the butter has hardened, pour off the liquid and discard it. Store the butter in a tightly sealed container in the refrigerator for up to 4 days or in the freezer for up to 6 months.

Oven-Roasted Tomatoes

Makes about 4 cups

These tomatoes will become a kitchen staple when you see how much punch and flavor they add to a vast number of dishes, including soups, sauces, fish, poultry, and meat. While you can make this with any sort of tomato, from hothouse to cherry to plum, the very best taste comes from making them from native (locally grown), in-season tomatoes, because they are the most flavorful.

You can make this recipe well ahead of time and keep the tomatoes in the refrigerator in a tightly covered container for several weeks. They also freeze beautifully in a tightly sealed container or freezer-strength reclosable plastic bag.

Preheat the oven to 400°F, with the rack in the upper third of the oven but not the highest position. Place the thyme on the bottom of a large roasting pan. Spread the tomatoes over the thyme, in one layer if possible. Drizzle with the olive oil, and sprinkle with the vinegar and salt. Bake for 45 minutes to 1 hour, or until the tomatoes have browned (unevenly) and given up their juices and the juices have reduced and become slightly thickened and syrupy. Allow the tomatoes to cool in the pan. Remove the thyme sprigs, if used, and either use the tomatoes immediately or store them in a tightly sealed container in the refrigerator.

4 large sprigs fresh thyme, or 2 teaspoons dried thyme leaves

5 pounds tomatoes, rinsed and cut into quarters (plum tomatoes can be cut in half, and cherry tomatoes can be left whole)

⅓ cup olive oil

3 tablespoons balsamic or red wine vinegar

2 teaspoons coarse salt

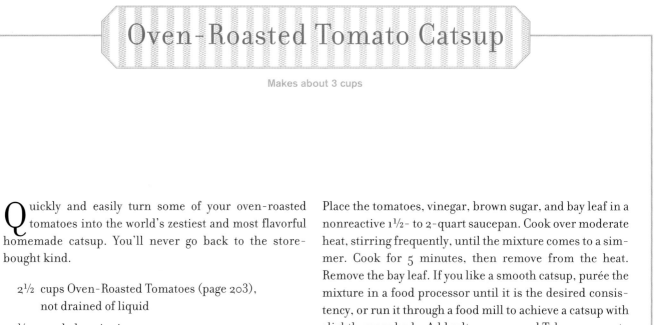

Oven-Roasted Tomato Catsup

Makes about 3 cups

Quickly and easily turn some of your oven-roasted tomatoes into the world's zestiest and most flavorful homemade catsup. You'll never go back to the store-bought kind.

2½ cups Oven-Roasted Tomatoes (page 203), not drained of liquid

¼ cup balsamic vinegar

¼ cup (packed) light brown sugar

1 bay leaf

Salt and freshly ground black pepper

Tabasco sauce

Place the tomatoes, vinegar, brown sugar, and bay leaf in a nonreactive 1½- to 2-quart saucepan. Cook over moderate heat, stirring frequently, until the mixture comes to a simmer. Cook for 5 minutes, then remove from the heat. Remove the bay leaf. If you like a smooth catsup, purée the mixture in a food processor until it is the desired consistency, or run it through a food mill to achieve a catsup with slightly more body. Add salt, pepper, and Tabasco sauce to taste. For a chunky catsup, simply mash it briefly with a potato masher. Refrigerate in a tightly sealed container for up to 3 months.

Pumpkin Cranberry Chutney

Makes 5 pints

My guess is that most Americans don't think about serving chutney unless they are making Indian food. Or, you eat it in a restaurant and think, Wow, this is good, but you don't go beyond taking out that bottle of Major Grey's Mango Chutney to perhaps spread on a smoked turkey sandwich. This beautiful and wonderfully flavorful concoction of brilliant orange pumpkin, accented by pinpoints of cranberry, will make you reach for the container much more often, adding an intriguingly international accent to all sorts of meat, poultry, fish, and game dishes. Don't forget to try it on a smoked turkey sandwich.

Not all pumpkins are good for cooking. Make sure you purchase a "sugar" pumpkin, one that has faint vertical green stripes and is a darker orange than its bound-for-jack-o'-lantern cousins.

1   1/2- to 3-pound sugar pumpkin, peeled, seeded, and cut into 1-inch pieces to yield 6 to 7 cups

2   large Granny Smith apples, scrubbed, cut in half, cored, and cut into 1/2-inch pieces

    Zest of 2 lemons, cut into medium julienne

    Juice of 2 lemons

1/4   cup peeled and grated ginger

1   large navel or other seedless orange, scrubbed, cut in half, and then sliced into 1/4-inch half-rounds

1/2   cup dried cranberries

2   or 3 red chile peppers, seeded and finely chopped

1   large sweet onion (such as Vidalia), peeled, cut in half, and then cut into 1/2-inch slices

1 1/2   cups (packed) dark brown sugar

1/2   cup pure maple syrup

1   tablespoon salt

2   tablespoons yellow mustard seed

1   teaspoon ground cloves

1   teaspoon ground cinnamon

4   cups orange juice

Place all the ingredients in a large, nonreactive pot set over medium-low heat. Stir to combine. Cover the pot, bring it to a gentle simmer, and cook, stirring frequently (but gently) for 50 to 60 minutes, or until most of the liquid is absorbed. Spoon into sterilized jars and seal according to the manufacturer's directions. Although you can eat the chutney now, the flavor will be better if you wait at least 2 weeks before serving.

Quick Fish Stock

Makes 2 cups

These days you can buy frozen fish stock, but it's really easy and a lot less expensive to make your own. If you are using fish frames (the bones left over after the fillets are cut off), be sure to ask the fishmonger to remove the gills. Fish stock freezes beautifully for up to 3 to 4 months when stored in a tightly sealed plastic container. It should not be kept in the refrigerator for more than 2 days.

2	tablespoons vegetable oil
1	medium onion, peeled and coarsely chopped
1	large carrot, peeled and cut into ¹/₂-inch slices
1	large stalk celery, cut into ¹/₂-inch slices
2	cloves garlic, peeled and crushed with the flat side of a chef's knife
1	cod or scrod fish frame, gills removed, or 1 pound cod or scrod, cut into 2-inch pieces
1	cup dry white wine
2¹/₂	cups water
1	teaspoon fennel seed
4	black peppercorns

Heat the oil in a large sauté pan set over moderate heat. Cook the onion, stirring frequently, until it is soft and golden. Add the carrot and celery and cook for another 5 minutes, stirring frequently. Add the garlic and cook for 1 minute more. Add the fish frames (cutting them into pieces, if necessary, to fit in the pan) or fish, wine, water, and seasonings. Bring the mixture to a gentle simmer and cook for 20 minutes, uncovered.

Strain through either a fine-mesh strainer or a strainer lined with cheesecloth, and refrigerate immediately until cold. Then freeze, if desired.

Simple Cranberry Sauce

Makes 1½ pints

Cranberry sauce isn't just for turkey at Thanksgiving. Either of the two following recipes is super on pancakes or waffles, used instead of mustard on a sandwich, or eaten right from the jar.

Fresh cranberries make a brief appearance in the supermarket a couple of weeks before Halloween and are around until Christmas. It's worth making this sauce with fresh berries if you can find them. I use organic cranberries that I buy fresh from a local farm stand to make this recipe, and I swear that the taste is better than the frozen packaged kind. Fresh cranberries don't keep for very long, so make the sauce as soon as possible after you buy the fruit (which has lots of natural pectin and is also a fabulous source of vitamin C). The cranberries look like semiliquid garnets suspended in ruby syrup.

1 pound (about 4 cups) fresh or frozen cranberries, picked over to remove any stems and moldy or shriveled berries

2 cups granulated sugar

Coarsely grated zest of 1 large, colorful orange

Place the cranberries, sugar, and zest in a nonreactive 3-quart saucepan set over medium heat. Stir to combine. Cook for 15 to 20 minutes, stirring frequently, until the sugar has dissolved and the cranberry skins pop open. Continue to cook, stirring frequently, until the juices have thickened. Spoon into sterilized canning jars and seal according to the manufacturer's directions, or freeze in tightly sealed containers.

Fresh Cranberry Orange Relish

Makes about 3 cups

There is good reason beyond their delicious taste to eat cranberries. Anyone prone to urinary tract infections should know that it has been scientifically proven that cranberries keep that culprit *E. coli* from adhering to the walls of the urinary tract. And there's more good news: Cranberries have five times the antioxidant content of broccoli (not to mention that they taste better), which means they have been shown to protect against cancer, stroke, and heart disease. According to studies done at the University of Scranton, this native American berry is able to decrease levels of total cholesterol and LDL (bad cholesterol) in animals. Studies are under way to see if the high levels of antioxidants in cranberries also protect against atherosclerosis.

The closer to fresh you eat cranberries, the better they are for you. Because very few people could stomach drinking straight cranberry juice, since it is so sour, the next best way is to eat them fresh with just enough sugar to balance the tartness. My friend Fern Fisher's recipe for Fresh Cranberry Orange Relish delivers just what you need.

2   cups fresh cranberries, picked over to remove any stems and moldy or shriveled berries

2   large, thick-skinned oranges

1   lime

1/2   cup (packed) dark brown sugar

1/3   cup pure maple syrup

1   cup toasted walnuts, coarsely chopped

1/4   cup crystallized ginger, finely chopped

Add the cranberries to a food processor fitted with the metal blade. Pulse to finely chop the berries. Remove the berries to a nonreactive bowl. Use a fine grater to grate the zest of the oranges and lime. Use a sharp knife to remove the white pith from the oranges and lime. Cut the orange pulp into several pieces, discarding any seeds, adding the pulp to the food processor. (Save the lime for the end.) Pulse to chop and add the chopped pulp and the zest to the cranberries. Stir in the brown sugar, maple syrup, walnuts, and ginger. If you like your cranberry sauce on the tart side, chop the lime pulp and add all or part of it to the mixture. Cover the bowl and refrigerate for several hours (or for as long as a week) before serving.

Index

A

Aïoli 80
Anago 174
Apples
  Dried Cranberry, Walnut,
    and Blue Cheese Salad 87
  Mulled Cider 182
  Pumpkin Cranberry Chutney 205
  Souffléd Apple Pancake 33
Asparagus, Roasted 95
Atlantic Spice House 78

B

Bacalhau (Portuguese Salt Cod) 116–17
Bacalhau with Fried Eggs 117
Baked Stuffed Clams 48
Baked Stuffed Lobster 128–29
Bananas
  Oatmeal Brûlée 40
Barnstable 19, 108
Baron, Jessica 49
Basil, shredding 89
Beach Plum Jam 194
Beans
  Kale Soup 68–69
  Quick White Bean and Garlic Dip 50
Beef
  Grilled Flank Steak 105
  New England Boiled Dinner 106
Beer
  Beer-Fried Oysters 133
  Lazy Man's Clambake 137
  New England Boiled Dinner 106
Beets
  Sunset Slaw 96
Berries. See also individual berries
  Cape Cod Scones 28
  Mixed Berry Shortcake 171
The Best Blueberry Muffins 29
Blackened Onion Relish 112–13
Blueberries
  The Best Blueberry Muffins 29
  Blueberry Pancakes 30–32
  Fresh Raspberry Blueberry Tart
    with a Shortbread Crust 155
Bluefish, Grilled, with
  Mustard and Lime 115

Boiled Lobster 130–31
Boiled Shrimp 57
Bonfire Mussels 141
Bourne 19
Bread
  Bread Bowl Salmon Chowder 81
  -crumbs, toasting 48
  Lobster Rolls 132
  Strawberries and Cream
    French Toast 42–43
Bread and Butter Pickles 196
Brewster 20, 22
Brody, Max 128
Broiled Gravlax 120–23
Brownies
  Chocolate Mint Brownies 160–61
  Mint Chip Brownie Ice
    Cream Sundae 161
Burgess, Thornton W. 19, 198, 199
Butter
  clarified 131
  Lobster Butter 201

C

Cabbage
  New England Boiled Dinner 106
  Sunset Slaw 96
Calamari Salad, Mac's 92
Candy Manor Hot Chocolate 185
Cape Cod Scones 28
Cape Cod Turnips 88
Cape Corn and Rice Salad 89
Caramelized Onion
  Mashed Potatoes 91
Catsup
  Cocktail Sauce 197
  Oven-Roasted Tomato Catsup 204
Cauliflower Flans 90
Chatham 19, 20, 185
Chatham Candy Manor 20, 185
Cheese. See also Cream cheese
  Bacalhau (Portuguese Salt Cod) 116–17
  Cauliflower Flans 90
  Dried Cranberry, Walnut,
    and Blue Cheese Salad 87
  Fresh Raspberry Blueberry
    Tart with a Shortbread Crust 155
  Smoked Salmon Cheesecake 62–63
  White Clam Pizza 148–49
Cheesecake
  Pumpkin Cheesecake 172
  Smoked Salmon Cheesecake 62–63
Chester Restaurant 169
Chicken
  Chicken Pot Pie 108–9
  Millie's Oven-Fried Chicken 114

Roasted Chicken with Oyster
    Cracker Stuffing 107
Child, Julia 128
Chocolate
  Candy Manor Hot Chocolate 185
  Chocolate-Covered Cape
    Cod Potato Chips 158–59
  Chocolate Crumb Crust 173
  Chocolate Mint Brownies 160–61
  Dune Cookies 162–63
  melting, 58, 159
  Mint Chip Brownie
    Ice Cream Sundae 161
  Quick and Easy Rocky
    Road Fudge 166
  Sand Dollars 156–57
  tempering 157
Chowders
  about 67
  Bread Bowl Salmon Chowder 81
  Clam Chowder 75–76
  P. J.'s Fish Chowder 73
Chutney, Pumpkin Cranberry 205
Cider, Mulled 182
Cilantro Pesto 124–25
Claiborne, Craig 62
Clambakes
  Lazy Man's Clambake 137
  Outdoor Clambake 134–36
Clams
  Baked Stuffed Clams 48
  Clam Chowder 75–76
  cleaning soft-shell 52
  Fried Clams 52
  Irma's Clam Fritters 49
  Lazy Man's Clambake 137
  Outdoor Clambake 134–36
  raw 54–55
  Sea Bass Poached in Ginger
    Fish Broth with Cilantro Pesto 124–25
  shucking 55
  Spaghetti with White Clam Sauce 146
  Steamed Clams 143
  varieties of 143
  White Clam Pizza 148–49
Classic Deviled Eggs 51
Coburn, Jay 169
Cocktail Sauce 197
Cod. See also Salt cod
  Cod Baked with
    Oven-Roasted Tomatoes 119
  Leslie Revsin's Sautéed Cod
    with Capers 139
  Quick Fish Stock 206
  Saffron-Scented Cod and
    Tomato Soup 78–80
Cook, Peter 68

Cookies
  Chocolate Mint Brownies   160–61
  Dune Cookies   162–63
Corn
  Cape Corn and Rice Salad   89
  Lazy Man's Clambake   137
  Outdoor Clambake   134–36
Cottage Street Bakery   35
Cottage Street Bakery Dirt Bombs   35–36
Crab
  Baked Stuffed Lobster   128–29
Cranberries
  Cranberry Martini   186
  Cranberry Orange Turkey Breast   110
  Cranberry-Pear Linzertorte   174–75
  Cranberry Salsa   200
  Dried Cranberry, Walnut, and
    Blue Cheese Salad   87
  Fresh Cranberry Orange Relish   208
  Grilled Pork with
    Cran-Asian Sauce   104
  health benefits of   208
  Pumpkin Cranberry Chutney   205
  Sea Breeze   180
  Simple Cranberry Sauce   207
Cream cheese
  Pumpkin Cheesecake   172
  Smoked Salmon Cheesecake   62–63
  Strawberries and Cream
    French Toast   42–43
Crème Brûlée Chester Restaurant,
  Lavender   169–70
Crow Farm   88
Crust, Chocolate Crumb   173
Cucumbers
  Bread and Butter Pickles   196
  Mac's Calamari Salad   92

D

Dennis   19
Desserts
  Chocolate-Covered Cape
    Cod Potato Chips   158–59
  Chocolate Mint Brownies   160–61
  Cranberry-Pear Linzertorte   174–75
  Dune Cookies   162–63
  Fresh Peach Ice Cream   164
  Fresh Raspberry Blueberry
    Tart with a Shortbread Crust   155
  Lavender Crème Brûlée
    Chester Restaurant   169–70
  Mint Chip Brownie
    Ice Cream Sundae   161
  Mixed Berry Shortcake   171
  Plum Kuchen   165
  Pumpkin Cheesecake   172

Quick and Easy Rocky
  Road Fudge   166
  Sand Dollars   156–57
Dillard, Annie   162
Dip, Quick White Bean and Garlic   50
Dried Cranberry, Walnut,
  and Blue Cheese Salad   87
Drinks
  Candy Manor Hot Chocolate   185
  Cranberry Martini   186
  Mulled Cider   182
  Red Snapper   180
  Red Tide   181
  Sea Breeze   180
  Sun Tea   189
Duck Breasts, Grilled Brined,
  with Blackened Onion Relish   112–13
Dune Cookies   162–63

E

Eastham   21, 22
Eggs
  Aïoli   80
  Bacalhau with Fried Eggs   117
  Classic Deviled Eggs   51
  Scrambled Eggs with Lox,
    Onions, and Peppers   37

F

Falmouth   19
First Encounter Beach   21
Fish
  Bacalhau (Portuguese Salt Cod)   116–17
  Bacalhau with Fried Eggs   117
  Cod Baked with Oven-Roasted
    Tomatoes   119
  Grilled Bluefish with Mustard
    and Lime   115
  Leslie Revsin's Sautéed Cod
    with Capers   139
  P. J.'s Fish Chowder,
    Quick Fish Stock   206
  Saffron-Scented Cod and
    Tomato Soup   78–80
  Sea Bass Poached in Ginger
    Fish Broth with Cilantro Pesto   124–25
  Slow-Cooked Striped Bass   127
Fisher, Fern   208
Flans, Cauliflower   90
Foley, Donna   88
Foriana Ciro and Sal's   144
Frankel, Mary   49
French Toast,
  Strawberries and Cream   42–43

Fresh Cranberry Orange Relish   208
Fresh Peach Ice Cream   164
Fresh Raspberry Blueberry
  Tart with a Shortbread Crust   155
Fried Clams   52
Fritters, Irma's Clam   49
Fudge, Quick and Easy Rocky Road   166

G

Ginger Pumpkin Bisque   70–72
Gravlax, Broiled   120–23
Gray, Sue   38
Green Briar Jam Kitchen   19, 198
Grilled Bluefish with Mustard
  and Lime   115
Grilled Brined Duck Breasts
  with Blackened Onion Relish   112–13
Grilled Flank Steak   105
Grilled Mussels   141
Grilled Pork with
  Cran-Asian Sauce   104
Grilled Sea Scallops
  (Scallop Kabobs)   138
Guerra, John   169

H

Hamel, P. J. and Rick   73
Harwich   19, 20
Hazelnuts
  Cranberry-Pear Linzertorte   174–75
  toasting   175
Herbes de Provence   63
Herring Cove Beach   47
Hickock, Pete   128
Hopper, Edward   20
Hultin, Linnet   78
Huntington, Cynthia   162
Hyannisport   21

I

Ice cream
  Fresh Peach Ice Cream   164
  Mint Chip Brownie
    Ice Cream Sundae   161
Irma's Clam Fritters   49

J

Jams
  See also Green Briar Jam Kitchen
  Beach Plum Jam   194
  Spiced Pear Jam   199
  Strawberry Jam   199

K

Kabobs, Scallop	138
Kale Soup	68–69
Keeley, Joanna	35
Kennedy, John F.	21
Kinkead, Bob	90
Kuchen, Plum	165

L

Lauterbach, Barbara	98
Lavender Crème Brûlée	
Chester Restaurant	169–70
Lazy Man's Clambake	137
Leighton, Mark	104
Lemons, zesting	59
Leslie Revsin's Sautéed Cod	
with Capers	139
Linzertorte, Cranberry-Pear	174–75
Lobster	
Baked Stuffed Lobster,	28–29
Boiled Lobster	130–31
Lazy Man's Clambake	137
Lobster Butter	201
Lobster Rolls	132
Outdoor Clambake	134–36
purchasing	130
size of	130
storing	130
Lox. See Salmon, smoked	

M

Macadamia nuts	
Dune Cookies	162–63
Mac's Calamari Salad	92
Mac's Seafood	92
Mailer, Norman	22, 144
Marshmallows	
Quick and Easy Rocky	
Road Fudge	166
Martini, Cranberry	186
Marty's	186
Mayflower Café	22
Mayo Duck Farm	112
Mayonnaise	
Aïoli	80
Tartar Sauce	197
Millie's Oven-Fried Chicken	114
Mint Chip Brownie	
Ice Cream Sundae	161
Mixed Berry Shortcake	171
Muffins	
The Best Blueberry Muffins	29
Cottage Street Bakery	
Dirt Bombs	35–36
Portuguese Muffins	38–39
Mulled Cider	182
Mushrooms	
Chicken Pot Pie	108–9
Mussels	
Bonfire Mussels	141
Classic Deviled Eggs	51
cleaning and debearding	60, 140
Grilled Mussels	141
Mussels Steamed with	
Wine and Garlic	140
Smoked Mussels	60

N

New England Boiled Dinner	106
Nuts. See also individual nuts	
Quick and Easy Rocky	
Road Fudge	166
Sand Dollars	156–57
toasting	167

O

Oatmeal	
leftover	41
Oatmeal Brûlée	40
Slow Cooker Oatmeal	41
Ojala Farm	108
Onions	
Blackened Onion Relish	112–13
Bread and Butter Pickles	196
Caramelized Onion	
Mashed Potatoes	91
New England Boiled Dinner	106
Sunset Slaw	96
Oranges	
Cranberry Orange Turkey Breast	110
Cranberry Salsa	200
Fresh Cranberry Orange Relish	208
Pumpkin Cranberry Chutney	205
Orleans	20, 35, 112
Outdoor Clambake	134–36
Oven-Roasted Tomato Catsup	204
Oven-Roasted Tomatoes	203
Oyster crackers	
Beer-Fried Oysters	133
Roasted Chicken with	
Oyster Cracker Stuffing	107
Oysters	
Beer-Fried Oysters	133
Classic Deviled Eggs	51
Oyster Stew	77
raw	54–55
shucking	55

P

Pamet Harbor	73
Pancakes	
Blueberry Pancakes	30–32
Souffléd Apple Pancake	33
Pasta. See Spaghetti	
Peach Ice Cream, Fresh	164
Pears	
Cranberry-Pear Linzertorte	174–75
Spiced Pear Jam	199
Peas	
Chicken Pot Pie	108–9
Two Salmon and Potato Salad	98
Pesto, Cilantro	124–25
Pickles	
Bread and Butter Pickles	196
Tartar Sauce	197
Pilgrims	21
Pizza, White Clam	148–49
P. J.'s Fish Chowder	73
Plums	
Beach Plum Jam	194
Plum Kuchen	165
Plymouth Colony Winery	104
Poached Salmon	99
Polombo, Joe	52
Pork, Grilled, with	
Cran-Asian Sauce	104
Portuguese Muffins	38–39
Portuguese Salt Cod (Bacalhau)	116–17
Potato Chips,	
Chocolate-Covered Cape Cod	158–59
Potatoes	
Bacalhau (Portuguese Salt Cod)	116–17
Bread Bowl Salmon Chowder	81
Caramelized Onion	
Mashed Potatoes	91
Clam Chowder	75–76
Kale Soup	68–69
New England Boiled Dinner	106
P. J.'s Fish Chowder	73
Roasted Potatoes	94
Sea Bass Poached in Ginger	
Fish Broth with Cilantro Pesto	124–25
Two Salmon and Potato Salad	98
Pot Pie, Chicken	108–9
Provincetown	19, 21, 22, 27, 47, 68, 144, 162, 169
Pumpkin	
Ginger Pumpkin Bisque	70–72
Pumpkin Cheesecake	172

Pumpkin Cranberry Chutney 205
  purée 72
  seeds, toasting 70

Q

Quick and Easy Rocky Road Fudge 166
Quick Fish Stock 206
Quick White Bean and Garlic Dip 50

R

Raspberry Blueberry Tart,
  Fresh, with a Shortbread Crust 155
Raw bar 54–55
Red Snapper 180
Red Tide 181
Relishes
  Blackened Onion Relish 112–13
  Fresh Cranberry Orange Relish 208
Revsin, Leslie 139
Rice Salad, Cape Corn and 89
Roasted Asparagus 95
Roasted Chicken with
  Oyster Cracker Stuffing 107
Roasted Potatoes 94
Rocky Road Fudge, Quick and Easy 166

S

Saffron
  Saffron-Scented Cod and
  Tomato Soup 78–80
  toasting 80
Salads
  Cape Corn and Rice Salad 89
  Dried Cranberry, Walnut,
    and Blue Cheese Salad 87
  Mac's Calamari Salad 92
  Sunset Slaw 96
  Two Salmon and Potato Salad 98
Salmon, fresh
  Bread Bowl Salmon Chowder 81
  Broiled Gravlax 120–23
  Poached Salmon 99
  Two Salmon and Potato Salad 98
Salmon, smoked
  Scrambled Eggs with Lox,
    Onions, and Peppers 37
  Smoked Salmon Cheesecake 62–63
  Two Salmon and Potato Salad 98
Salsa, Cranberry 200
Salt cod
  Bacalhau (Portuguese Salt Cod) 116–17
  Bacalhau with Fried Eggs 117
Sand Dollars 156–57

Sandwich 19, 88, 198
Sauces
  Cocktail Sauce 197
  Simple Cranberry Sauce 207
  Tartar Sauce 197
  White Clam Sauce 146
Sausage
  Kale Soup 68–69
  Outdoor Clambake 134–36
Scallops
  Grilled Sea Scallops
    (Scallop Kabobs) 138
  removing muscle from 59
  Scallop Seviche 58–59
Scones, Cape Cod 28
Scrambled Eggs with Lox,
  Onions, and Peppers 37
Sea Bass Poached in Ginger
  Fish Broth with Cilantro Pesto 124–25
Sea Breeze 180
Shortcake, Mixed Berry 171
Shrimp
  Boiled Shrimp 57
  Outdoor Clambake 134–36
Simple Cranberry Sauce 207
Simple Syrup 189
Slaw, Sunset 96
Slow-Cooked Striped Bass 127
Slow Cooker Oatmeal 41
Smoked Mussels 60
Smoked Salmon Cheesecake 62–63
Souffléd Apple Pancake 33
Soups. See also Chowders
  Ginger Pumpkin Bisque 70–72
  Kale Soup 68–69
  Saffron-Scented Cod and
    Tomato Soup 78–80
  in slow cookers 72
Spaghetti
  Spaghetti Foriana Ciro and Sal's 144
  Spaghetti with White Clam Sauce 146
Spiced Pear Jam 199
Spinach
  Dried Cranberry, Walnut,
    and Blue Cheese Salad 87
Squid
  Mac's Calamari Salad 92
Steamed Clams 143
Stew, Oyster 77
Stock, Quick Fish 206
Strawberries
  Strawberries and Cream
    French Toast 42–43
  Strawberry Jam 199
Striped Bass, Slow-Cooked 127
Sundae, Mint Chip Brownie
  Ice Cream 161

Sunset Slaw 96
Sun Tea 189
Sweet potatoes
  Ginger Pumpkin Bisque 70–72

T

Tartar Sauce 197
Tarts
  Cranberry-Pear Linzertorte 174–75
  Fresh Raspberry Blueberry
    Tart with a Shortbread Crust 155
Tea, Sun 189
Tomatoes
  Cod Baked with
    Oven-Roasted Tomatoes 119
  Oven-Roasted Tomato Catsup 204
  Oven-Roasted Tomatoes 203
  Red Snapper 180
  Saffron-Scented Cod and
    Tomato Soup 78–80
  Sea Bass Poached in Ginger
    Fish Broth with Cilantro Pesto 124–25
Truro 20, 22, 78
Turkey
  Cranberry Orange Turkey Breast 110
  Turkey Pot Pie 108–9
Turner, Naomi 185
Turnips, Cape Cod 88
Two Salmon and Potato Salad 98

V

Veach, David 185
Vodka
  Cranberry Martini 186
  Red Tide 181
  Sea Breeze 180

W

Walnuts
  The Best Blueberry Muffins 29
  Dried Cranberry, Walnut,
    and Blue Cheese Salad 87
  Fresh Cranberry Orange Relish 208
  Spaghetti Foriana Ciro and Sal's 144
Wellfleet 20, 38,
  73, 92
  130, 131
White, Jasper
White Clam Pizza 148–49
Wiebusch, Alice 174

Table of Equivalents

The exact equivalents in the following table have been rounded for convenience.

Liquid/Dry Measures

U.S.		Metric
¼	teaspoon	1.25 milliliters
½	teaspoon	2.5 milliliters
1	teaspoon	5 milliliters
1	tablespoon (3 teaspoons)	15 milliliters
1	fluid ounce (2 tablespoons)	30 milliliters
¼	cup	60 milliliters
⅓	cup	80 milliliters
½	cup	120 milliliters
1	cup	240 milliliters
1	pint (2 cups)	480 milliliters
1	quart (4 cups, 32 ounces)	960 milliliters
1	gallon (4 quarts)	3.84 liters
1	ounce (by weight)	28 grams
1	pound	454 grams
2.2	pounds	1 kilogram

Length

U.S.	Metric
⅛ inch	3 millimeters
¼ inch	6 millimeters
½ inch	12 millimeters
1 inch	2.5 centimeters

Oven Temperature

Fahrenheit	Celsius	Gas
250	120	½
275	140	1
300	150	2
325	160	3
350	180	4
375	190	5
400	200	6
425	220	7
450	230	8
475	240	9
500	260	10